LANGUAGE IN
THE PHILOSOPHY
OF ARISTOTLE

by

SISTER MIRIAM THERESE LARKIN, C.S.J.

1971

MOUTON

THE HAGUE · PARIS

185
C
⅃ 324

147115

Printed in The Netherlands by Mouton & Co., Printers, The Hague.

*For my family
and my community*

PREFACE

This book examines Aristotle's theory of philosophical language in the light of his theory of signification. Although meaning, for Aristotle, is the property of a word whereby it arrests the attention and communicates understanding, Aristotle is not primarily interested in meaning in this general sense but rather in the meaning of nouns and verbs as they are the subjects and predicates of enunciations. Aristotle then in treating language is not interested in constructing a grammar of language. An examination of the *De Interpretatione*, the *Poetics*, and the *Rhetoric* substantiates my view that Aristotle is not interested in grammar.

I attempt to determine what constitutes philosophical language for Aristotle by examining and comparing poetical, rhetorical, dialectical and demonstrative arguments. Aristotle's critique of his predecessors on language throws further light on his theory of philosophical language. Chapter five examines an instance of Aristotle's use of language in order to exemplify how he was concerned not solely with linguistic clarification but with linguistic clarification *as ordered to* knowledge of reality.

An earlier version of this book constituted part of my dissertation for the Ph. D. degree in philosophy which was received at the University of Notre Dame in June, 1965. I would like to acknowledge my indebtedness to the following philosophers for their comments and criticisms: Joseph Bobik, James C. Doig, Guido Kung, Harry Nielson. I would also like to express my gratitude to Ralph M. McInerny who inspired me to the greated extent in this work. Finally, I am grateful to Teresa M. Dunbar without whose secretarial assistance the completion of this work would not have been possible.

Los Angeles, California   Sister Miriam Therese Larkin, C.S.J.
May 7, 1970

TABLE OF CONTENTS

Preface   5

1. Introduction   9

2. Aristotle's Theory of Signification 13
   2.1 Introduction 13
   2.2 Plato and Language 14
   2.3 What is Language?. 18
   2.4 The Use of Language 19
   2.5 Meaning or Signification 21
       2.5.1 Convention 22
       2.5.2 The Meaning of Sentences. 25
       2.5.3 The Meaning of Parts of Sentences 27
             2.5.3.1 The Noun 28
             2.5.3.2 The Verb. 30
             2.5.3.3 Summary. 33
   2.6 Reference. 34
   2.7 Language: Grammar or Logic? 35
   2.8 Signification of General Terms 40
   2.9 Conclusion . . . . . . : 43

3. Philosophical Language 45
   3.1 Introduction 45
       3.1.1 The Problem. 46
       3.1.2 Hesiod and Empedocles 46
   3.2 The Language of Proof. 49
       3.2.1 Proofs 50

8   TABLE OF CONTENTS

3.2.2 Clarity and the Language of Proofs 54
    3.2.2.1 Rhetoric and Poetry 55
    3.2.2.2 Demonstration and Dialectic 61
3.2.3 Confusion of Meaning: The Sophists; Plato . . 62
3.2.4 Metaphors; Plato: Empedocles. 64
3.2.5 Words Said in Many Ways 67
    3.2.5.1 *Pròs Hén* Equivocals 67
    3.2.5.2 The Meaning of Metaphor 72
    3.2.5.3 The Division of Words 75
3.3 Conclusion 76

4. A Use of Language: The Meaning of "Being" 77
4.1 Introduction 77
4.2 Aristotle's Purpose in Metaphysics 80
4.3 The Meanings of "Being". 82
  4.3.1 Accidental Being and True Being 82
  4.3.2 Essential Being: Being of the Categories. . . . 84
4.4 The Referent of "Being" 88
4.5 Conclusion 90
Appendix: The Subject of Metaphysics 91

5. Summary and Conclusion 95
5.1 Theory of Signification 95
5.2 Philosophical Language. 98
5.3 A Use of Language: The Meaning of "Being" 102

Bibliography 105

Index. 109

1

INTRODUCTION

The aim of this study is to examine Aristotle's theory of signification as well as certain arguments he uses in order to delineate his
theory of philosophical language. In the literature on Aristotelian
philosophy, there is no work devoted to a study of his theory of
language in general or of philosophical language. In recent literature there appears some criticism, although not of a substantial
nature, of the function of language in Aristotle's philosophy. Such,
for instance, is the argument that discourse is the foundation of
metaphysics, that without any sensible or intellectual intuition of
being *qua* being any philosophy of being is a philosophy of the
meanings of "being".[1]

Margaret Macdonald refers to Aristotle, among other philosophers, as using "what men say" as the criteria for the truth and
falsity of philosophical propositions. Since, according to Miss Macdonald, these propositions are formulated in words used analogous-
ly but not intelligibly, the propositions of philosophy are non-
significant. They do not tell us about reality.[2] Another tributary
to theories about the function of language contends that the object
of Aristotle's investigations is extra-linguistic reality, but that his
method of philosophical analysis is negative and therapeutic, directly removing misleading interpretations of the facts of experience while only indirectly explicating truths without explaining,

---

[1]   Pierre Aubenque, *Le problème de l'être chez Aristote* (Paris: Presses Universitaires de France, 1962), p. 235.
[2]   "The Philosopher's Use of Analogy", *Logic and Language*. Edited by
Antony Flew (Oxford: Basil Blackwell, 1955), pp. 80-100.

proving or justifying these truths. Nothing positive about reality is stated.[3]

Aristotle, arriving on the philosophical scene after Plato, changes the nature of the philosophical question about language and reality. For Plato and earlier philosophers, the theory of a natural relation between names and things named had been entertained for a time.[4] Aristotle's theory of conventional signification changes the nature of the question. No longer is the relation between words and things considered a natural one. Aristotle still intends, however, to obtain knowledge of reality and appears to depend on language in doing so.

That it is Aristotle's intention to speak about reality in doing philosophy cannot be questioned. In *Sophistical Refutations* Aristotle notes that a confusion of names with things causes error in reasoning: "...it is impossible to argue by introducing the actual things under discussion, but we use names as symbols in the place of things...".[5] The reason for using names is that we cannot calculate with the things themselves. He claims that metaphysics, the highest wisdom, is concerned with the rational knowledge of ultimate principles and factors: "Clearly, then, wisdom is rational knowledge concerning certain basic factors and principles."[6] It is in this endeavor that he sees himself in continuity with his predecessors: "Let us, nevertheless, here appeal for confirmation to our predecessors in this inquiry into beings and in philosophizing about what is true concerning them. For clearly they, too, speak of principles and ultimate factors."[7]

On the other hand, Aristotle is engaged so frequently in an analysis of the terms he uses that a simple perusal of his writings could suggest the premature conclusion that in doing philosophy he is merely clarifying terms. In the *Metaphysics*, for example, he analyzes being by examining the meanings of "being".[8] This, of course,

[3]   Maxwell John Charlesworth, *Philosophy and Linguistic Analysis* (Pittsburg: Duquesne University Press, 1959), pp. 210-215.
[4]   See Plato's *Cratylus*.
[5]   Ch. 1: 165a6-7. Cf. *Topics* I: ch. 18; 102a21; *Met*.IV: ch. 4; 1006b22.
[6]   *Met*. I: ch. 1; 982a2.
[7]   *Ibid*., ch. 3; 983b-5.
[8]   *Ibid*., IV: ch. 1, 2; also VII: ch. 4; 1029b13-1030a27; V: ch. 7.

inclines one immediately to agree with Aubenque's thesis that philosophy of being is merely an examination of the meanings of "being". The fifth book of the *Metaphysics* is entirely devoted to the meanings of words. One might question, also, whether Aristotle's arguments from the way men speak can lead to any positive knowledge of reality. The cursory and tangential approaches to this question in the recent literature and the resulting variety of theories, as well as the at least superficially apparent ambiguities in Aristotle's works, raise questions that demand a more substantial treatment of the subject.

This study is an initial step in this important subject. It centers on the question: What constitutes philosophical language for Aristotle, and does Aristotle, in depending on language in philosophy, merely clarify language or provide positive knowledge of reality? If Aristotle does succeed in arriving at a positive knowledge, we will want to know (a) what kind of language does he allow in doing philosophy, and (b) how, through language, does he arrive at positive knowledge?

Because Aristotle rejects the theory of a natural relation between names and things named and yet attempts to attain knowledge of reality through language, the second chapter of this work will treat Aristotle's theory of signification in order to determine how, for Aristotle, words relate to things and in which way words have meaning in philosophy. Once we have examined the works in which Aristotle treats signification of names, we will be in a position to determine the possibility of Aristotle's being concerned only with grammar, that is, with satisfying the conventional rules of correctness in speech so that men, in communicating, may understand each other. Although Aristotle has not explicitated a theory of reference, it will be necessary in the second chapter to determine what would constitute his theory of reference.

Chapter Three will consider the specifications beyond his theory of signification that Aristotle makes regarding philosophical language. He refers to the language of philosophy as the "language of proof" as distinct from the subtle language of the mythologists, Homer and Hesiod. To understand what he means by language of proof will involve an investigation of the kinds of proofs Aristotle admits in philosophy as well as the kind of language admitted in these proofs and the possible reasons for using this kind of language.

Although Aristotle refuses to admit verbal arguments directed only to names, he seems at times to use what we may call linguistic arguments. Chapter Four will examine Aristotle's actual use of the way men speak to obtain knowledge of reality. A complete examination of this question would be a gargantuan task, more than the nature of this work will allow. We will confine our study to an example which we think is particularly relevant to the problem of attaining knowledge of reality — the linguistic criterion of the unity of metaphysics — being said in many ways. It is our purpose here to indicate that being *qua* being, according to Aristotle, has a non-linguistic foundation in reality. In doing this we will rely chiefly on an examination of *Metaphysics IV*, chapter two, and *V*, chapter seven.

2

ARISTOTLE'S THEORY OF SIGNIFICATION

2.1 INTRODUCTION

Aristotle doubtlessly would agree with Socrates' contention that "the knowledge of names is a great part of knowledge",[1] but his reason for saying this would differ from that of Socrates. For Plato and earlier philosophers, one of the commonly held theories of language was that names were naturally related to things named. Aristotle with his theory of conventional names rejected the earlier theory of Plato. Aristotle intended to attain knowledge of reality. But Plato would object that if there is no natural relation of names to things, how can language tell us about reality? In order to pursue this problem we will, in this chapter, examine how words have meaning for Aristotle and in what sense meaning is relevant in philosophy.

We will then be in a position to take the first steps in determining whether Aristotle in treating language was simply concerned with establishing the rules of grammar so that men, in communicating, may understand each other. This will be done by examining his more formal treatises on language.

Finally, because it is with language in philosophy that we are concerned, the last part of this chapter will indicate, in the light of what philosophy is, what kinds of sentences and meaning are relevant for philosophy.

[1] *Cratylus*, 384B.

2.2 PLATO AND LANGUAGE

We have mentioned that Aristotle rejects Plato's hypothesis of the natural relation of names to things named. Before turning to Aristotle's theory of meaning, let us examine the path by which Plato arrives at his disillusionment with names as sources of knowledge and introduces the theory of conventional names.

For Plato, the problem of names was part of the problem of the possibility of knowledge of things as they are. This becomes evident in the *Cratylus* and in *Letter VII*. In the dialogue Plato, through Socrates, argues at first for a theory of natural names which may be true or false according as they represent the thing named. Socrates gives three arguments for the possibility of natural names which are false. (1) False names are parts of false propositions.[2] (2) Naming is an action; just as things have a naturally prescribed relation to their essence, so actions, including naming which is a part of speaking, have a natural relation to the natural process of speaking.[3] (3) Naming is an instrument of teaching and distinguishing natures; therefore names must be naturally related to those things which they name.[4]

According to Socrates, there is a skilled name-legislator who knows "how to put the true natural name of each thing into sound and syllables, and to make and give all names with a view to the ideal name, if he is to be a namer in any true sense".[5] What is this true natural or ideal name without sound or syllables to which the legislator must look for his model? Since it is without materials of sound and syllables, it must be the form of the name, which seems to mean the essence of the thing.

If it is true that names are naturally related to that which they name, Socrates must undertake to demonstrate this. He does so

[2] 385B.

[3] 386A-387D.

[4] Socrates erroneously assumes that speaking is the same kind of physical action as weaving and that the name is an instrument like the awl. To speak, one must use the instrument naturally fitted for the action, i.e. the name. Actually the natural instruments for speaking or naming are the human intellect and certain physical organs. Socrates uses this argument to avoid names' being relative to the one who names. Cf. *De Int.* ch. 4: 16b34.

[5] 389A-E.

by an examination of the etymology of the names of immutable essences — gods, stars and elements of the universe, and virtues.[6] This examination seems to verify the Heraclitean theory of the flux of the universe since many names originally designated rivers or things in motion. Socrates explains that the original name-givers probably became dizzy in their search for names and so interpreted the universe as always in motion. Since the forms of many names have been radically altered, to be more exact in this examination of names it is necessary to examine the primary elements of names and their relation to the natures of things.[7] Because a name is an imitation made by letters and syllables, it is necessary to separate letters into classes to ascertain whether the namer has used a simple letter to denote a simple thing.[8] If this does not prove to be so, then the gods and barbarians must have given names, and antiquity has cast a veil over the original names.

This examination, however, disappoints Socrates who begins to distrust his own view of natural names.[9] He maintains the theory of names as images: names and their letters retain sufficient likeness to the object to be vehicles of intelligent communication; but this theory must be supplemented by convention and custom. Letters having no likeness to the object can still indicate the object since they are sanctioned by custom.[10]

And what is custom but convention? I utter a sound which I understand, and you know that I understand the meaning of the sound: ... and if when I speak you know my meaning, there is an indication given by me to you ... This indication of my meaning may proceed from unlike as well as from like ... But if this is true, then you have made a convention with yourself, and the correctness of a name turns out to be convention. And even supposing that you must distinguish custom from convention ever so much, still you must say that the signification of words is given by custom and not by likeness, for custom may indicate by the unlike as well as by the like. But as we are agreed thus far, Cratylus, ... then custom and convention must be supposed to contribute to the indication of our thoughts.[11]

6   397A-411A.
7   422D.
8   424C.
9   428B.
10   435B-D.
11   435A ff.

Socrates acknowledges that the "dragging in of resemblance" is a shabby thing.[12] He does no more, however, than to say that convention must supplement it.

Cratylus agrees with Socrates that names are not only the source of information and instruction but also the means of inquiry and discovery.[13] For Socrates, this means that he who follows names in the search after things and analyzes their meanings is in danger of being deceived, for the first namegiver may have been deceived in his conception of things, or may, as the analysis of names has already indicated, have been inconsistent in naming things according to the first principles of naming.[14] Another argument against Cratylus's theory that things are known through names is the problem of how the first namegiver could have known things since there could not have been prior names through which he could have known things. If, on the other hand, the gods gave names, they acted according to contradictory first principles since some names express motion and some rest. Socrates concludes that because names do not give a consistent picture of things, recourse must be had to another standard for knowing the truth of things without employing names.[15] The only possibility, or course, is to know the things themselves. Cratylus admits that it is nobler to learn from the truth whether the truth and the image of it have been duly executed than to learn from the image. Socrates then leads Cratylus to admit that there must be absolute Forms since, if things are always in flux, it would be impossible to know them: "there will be no one to know and nothing to be known". Whether there is an eternal nature in things or whether things are in flux, is difficult to determine. But

no man of sense will like to put himself or the education of his mind in the power of names: neither will he so far trust names or the givers of names as to be confident in any knowledge which condemns himself and other existences to an unhealthy state of unreality.[16]

---

[12]   435D.
[13]   435D-436A.
[14]   436B-F.
[15]   438A-D.
[16]   440C.

Once Socrates has limited natural fitness to the names of immutable essences, truth and falsity of names is defined in terms of representation of the essences of things. The examination of the etymology of names proves that names do not exactly represent what and how things really are. The theory of imitation is not completely rejected but must be supplemented by convention; with this admission attention is drawn to speech as a means of communicating meaning rather than as an action. With the failure of the imitation theory of names arises the distrust of achieving knowledge of things through names; it is the possibility of achieving knowledge of things as they are that appears to be Plato's basic problem.

Because of the admission of convention in naming, Plato's confidence in names as sources of knowledge is weakened. In *Letter VII*, Plato voices his belief in the inadequacy of language more strongly. According to him, knowledge of real objects (Forms) comes through names, descriptions, and images which may be drawn and erased on the lathe and which do not affect the real objects. But knowledge and understanding of real objects is not found in sounds nor in shapes but in minds; names, descriptions, bodily forms, and concepts do as much to illustrate the particular quality of any object as they do to illustrate its essential reality because of the inadequacy of language.

Hence no intelligent man will ever be so bold as to put into language those things which his reason has contemplated, especially not into a form that is unalterable — which must be the case with what is expressed in written symbols.[17]

True knowledge, according to Plato, requires an inborn affinity with the subject. Without this affinity there is not the slightest possibility of true knowledge.

Hardly after practicing detailed comparisons of names and definitions and visual and other sense perceptions, after scrutinizing them in benevolent disputation by the use of question and answer without jealousy, at last in a flash understanding of each blazes up, and the mind, as it exerts all its powers to the limit of human capacity, is flooded with light.[18]

[17]   342E-343A.
[18]   344B.

No serious man, therefore, will even write about serious realities for the general public.

In a word, it is an inevitable conclusion from this that when anyone sees any-where the written work of anyone, whether that of a lawgiver in his laws or whatever it may be in some other form, the subject treated cannot have been his most serious concern — that is, if he is himself a serious man.[19]

But Aristotle, having rejected the belief in separate Forms, will have a different theory of the nature of names.

2.3   WHAT IS LANGUAGE?

To what does Aristotle refer when he speaks of language as he is concerned with it? The natural basis of language is voice or articu-late sound (φωνή). Voice is distinguished from articulate speech (διάλεκτος) and from the noise produced by the movement of air (ψόφος)[20] which is its natural basis in sound. Voice is the material of speech and man alone of all the animals uses voice in speech.[21]

Although sound is made by any movement of air,[22] voice is sound with meaning dependent on man's possession of special organs whose operation is a function of the soul.[23] The pharynx, teeth, tongue, and lips function in the production of articulate sound.[24] Materially, then, language is the combination of sounds called letters produced in voice by pharynx, lips, teeth, and tongue. Some animals, with voice, have the power to articulate sounds and to signify pleasure and pain.[25] But language — the power of con-versation or speech — is proper only to man by reason of his in-

---

[19]   344C.
[20]   *Hist. An.* IV: ch. 9; 535a26.
[21]   *De Gen. An.* V: ch. 7; 786b19-22.
[22]   *De Anima* II: ch. 8; 420a3-19; *De Sensu*, 440b27.
[23]   *De Anima* II: ch. 8; 420b4-421a6.
[24]   *De Part. An.* II: ch. 16-17; 659b21-660b11; III: ch. 1; 661a34-b17; *De Gen. An.* V: ch. 8; 788b3-9; *Hist. An.* II: ch. 12; 504b1-3; *Problemata* X: ch. 39; XI: ch. 57; 905a30-34.
[25]   *Pol.* I: ch. 2; 1253a10. Aristotle elsewhere indicates that animals have some power to communicate, to give and receive instruction. Cf. *De Part. An.* II: ch. 17; 660a35-b2; *Hist. An.* IX: ch. 1; 608a17.

telligence, for while the capability of speech implies the capability of uttering vocal sounds, the converse is not true.

We may define language, then, as the expression of meaning in words.[26] Rational speech differs from that of animals in that its significance depends on the operation of human intelligence.[27] All men as members of the same species possess the same range of vocal sounds and agree in the use of vocal sounds to convey meanings; but they differ from each other in the forms of language.[28]

2.4 THE USE OF LANGUAGE

As we have seen, the power of speech differentiates men from animals who have only voice which is significant of their pleasures and pains. Since, according to Aristotle, nature operates for a determinate end, the power of speech which is naturally a power of human beings is ordered to the end of understanding and communication. It is difficult to say whether Aristotle thinks men are social because they have the power of speech or the converse. At any rate he sees the need for virtuous men to live together to share discussion and thought by means of language.[29] The object of understanding and communication varies according as the use of the rational principle does. Since for Aristotle thinking is either practical, artistic, or theoretical,[30] the use of language will vary according as thought does.

Aristotle holds that the purpose of speech in practical matters is to signify the useful and the injurious, the just and the unjust,

---

[26] *Poetics* ch. 6: 1450b14.
[27] Aristotle refers to rational speech in various places as διάλεκτον — the speech of ordinary conversation; ερμηνεία — language or interpretation; λογος — language or rational speech; ὄνομα — name, principles of enunciation; φωνός σημάντικη — significant sound.
[28] *Hist. An.* IV: ch. 9; 536b8-20; *Prob.* X: ch. 39; 895a7-14; XI: ch. 1; 898b30-899a3.
[29] *Nich. Eth.* IX: ch. 9; 1170b9-14.
[30] *Met.* VI: ch. 1; 1025b18-26; *Topics* VI: ch. 6; 145a15-18; *Nich. Eth.* II: ch. 2; 1103b26-29; ch. 4; 1140a2.

about which only man has knowledge.[31] This possibility of communication among men is the basis for domestic and civil societies; man is naturally a domestic and political animal.

But the desire of men for knowledge is not confined to knowledge of the useful, or good and bad actions; not every man is destined to live solely at the practical level. Given leisure from practical affairs, the wise man who knows the reason for all things, even the most difficult, and who is interested in knowledge for its own sake, is superior to the man who lives at the practical level.[32] Just as the man of politics is concerned with the useful and injurious in human actions, so the wise man is concerned with theoretical knowledge, with rational knowledge concerning certain basic factors and principles.[33] In like manner, just as the man of practical affairs uses language to express and to communicate with others about what is good and bad, so the wise man uses language to signify basic factors and principles of things and to communicate this knowledge.[34]

Finally, the product of artistic thought is poetry, the imitation of things as they are or ought to be.[35] It is the language in poetry

[31]   "... the power of speech is intended to set forth the expedient and inexpedient, and therefore likewise the just and the unjust. And it is characteristic of man that he alone has any sense of good and evil, of just and unjust, and the like, and the association of living beings who have this sense makes a family and a state." *Pol.* I: ch. 2; 1253a12-18.

[32]   "And this activity alone would seem to be loved for its own sake; for nothing arises from it apart from the contemplating, while from practical activities we gain more or less apart from the action. And happiness is thought to depend on leisure; for we are busy that we may have leisure, and make war that we may live in peace." *Nich. Eth.* X: ch. 7; 1177a29-1177b2.

[33]   *Met.* I: ch. 2; 981b28:982a4.

[34]   "For while a philosopher, as well as a just man or one possessing any other virtue, needs the necessaries of life, when they are sufficiently equipped with things of that sort the just man needs people towards whom and with whom he shall act justly, and the temperate man, the brave man, and each of the others is in the same case, but the philosopher, even when by himself, can contemplate truth, and the better the wiser he is; he can perhaps do so better if he has fellow-workers, but still he is the most self-sufficient." *Nich. Eth.* X: ch. 7; 1177b2-6.

[35]   "Tragedy is, then, a representation of an action that is heroic and complete and of a certain magnitude — by means of language enriched with all kinds of ornament, each used separately in the different parts of the play: it represents

that relates the thoughts of the character to his action and presents the action of the plot.[36] But language in poetry depends on more than meaning to achieve its effect; sound and rhythm are important considerations in the production of the artistic effect.[37]

These, then, are the uses of language for Aristotle. Such uses determine his verbal arts of logic, rhetoric, and poetics respectively. It is to these arts that we turn for his theory of signification.

2.5 MEANING OR SIGNIFICATION

In order to give language its foundation in thought or intelligence, Aristotle speaks of the signification of words as follows:

Spoken words are the symbols (σύμβολα) of mental experience and written words are the symbols of spoken words. Just as all men have not the same writing, so all men have not the same speech sounds, but the mental experiences, which these directly symbolize, are the same for all, as also are those things of which our experiences are the images.[38]

According to St. Thomas, the passions of the soul or mental experiences may refer to any of the operations by which the soul is affected — either the image of the imagination or the understanding of the possible intellect.[39] These passions of the soul and the things of which these are the likenesses are, in any given case, the same for all, for many words even in different languages may stand for one thought about one thing. The states of the soul are by themselves resemblances of the things with which they correspond while

---

men in action and does not use narrative, and through pity and fear it effects relief to these and similar emotions." *Poetics* ch. 6: 1449b21-28.

[36] "Under the head of Thought come all the effects to be produced by the language. Some of these are proof and refutation, the arousing of feelings like pity, fear, anger, and so on, and then again exaggeration and depreciation." *Ibid.*, ch. 19; 1456a36-1456b1.

[37] "By 'language enriched' I mean that which has rhythm and tune, e.g. song, and by 'the kinds separately' I mean that some effects are produced by verse alone and some again by song ... By 'diction' I mean here the metrical arrangement of the words; and 'songmaking' I use in the full, obvious sense of the word." *Ibid.*, ch. 6: 1449b28-31; b34-36.

[38] *De Int.* ch. 1: 16a3-7.

[39] *In De Int.* less. 1; #6.

words do not naturally by themselves resemble the thing they represent. Just as no word has a necessary relation to a thought, no written symbol has a natural relation to a particular sound; hence the possibility of synonyms, homonyms, different languages and different alphabets. The brevity of Aristotle's explanation here indicates that he is introducing the point that language refers to things through thought. It is not merely a communication with someone but communication *of* something *to* someone. In other words, the relation or reference of words to things is not natural but conventional.

2.5.1 *Convention*

Aristotle would agree with Socrates of the *Cratylus* that the "dragging in of resemblance" between names and things to explain the meaning of words "is a shabby device".[40] Aristotle speaks of words as symbols; that is, they are significant by the conventions of men.

By a noun we mean a sound significant by convention... The limitation 'by convention' was introduced because nothing is by nature a noun or name — it is only so when it becomes a symbol; inarticulate sounds, such as those which brutes produce, are significant yet none of these constitutes a noun.[41]

Every sentence has meaning, not as being the natural means by which a physical faculty is realized but as we have said, by convention.[42]

This is Aristotle's answer to the problem of natural names in the *Cratylus*[43] where the attempt is made by Socrates to show that

[40]   435D.
[41]   *De Int.* ch. 2: 16a19-29.
[42]   *Ibid.*, ch. 4: 17a1-2. The Greek language had only one word, ὄνομα, where English has "word", "name", "noun". "Name" in the English translations and in our text is the equivalent of "word". Aristotle is equating naming with saying, but not in the modern sense of naming which implies denotation of an entity.
[43]   Aubenque, *op. cit.*, p. 106, claims that Aristotle's theory of language is in direct answer to the Sophists, not to Plato. I disagree, however, for the entire *De Interpretatione* can be seen as a counterpart of the *Sophist*. Aristotle's theory of signification answers Plato's problem in the *Cratylus*. Aristotle's theory differs from Plato's theory of imitation chiefly because Aristotle rejected the doctrine of Forms.

names are natural because a name is an instrument of the act of naming, of teaching and distinguishing natures; therefore it must be naturally related to that which it names. Note that for Aristotle natural inarticulate sounds designate but do not signify. From such inarticulate sounds we may learn the desires and states of emotion of both men and beasts, but only lettered names are symbols, constituted with a definite meaning by the intelligence of men.

The name is not a natural sound of man or beast and neither is it the direct instrument of a natural power. The throat, lungs, tongue, teeth, lips are instruments for producing names which are the artificial effects of the use of these instruments by intelligent beings.[44] Although names are thought of as effects of speech or communication, it is only because of the intervention of the intellect in imposing names and in using them that a name has any relation to that which it names. In saying that names are conventional and not natural, Aristotle means that letters and syllables have no necessary natural likeness to that which they signify. Yet they can still refer to reality by intervention of the intellect. This theory of conventionality of names is well expressed at the end of the *Cratylus*:

... custom may indicate by the unlike as well as by the like ... custom and convention must be supposed to contribute to the indication of our thoughts ...[45]

I utter a sound which I understand, and you know that I understand the meaning of the sound ... and if when I speak you know my meaning, there is an indication given by me to you.[46]

Aristotle, having dropped the belief in the existence of Forms, or ideal names, can refer names to thought and through thought to sensible things. Intelligence provides the possibility of conventional names.

Ackrill, in his commentary on *De Interpretatione*, objects to Aristotle's claim that names are conventional.[47] The statement

[44] *In De Int.*, less. 6; #80, 81.
[45] 435B-C.
[46] 434E-435A.
[47] *Aristotle's Categories and De Interpretatione*, trans. J. L. Ackrill (Oxford: At the Clarendon Press, 1963), p. 117.

that brute inarticulate sounds are not names because they are not articulate does not prove, according to Ackrill, that names must be conventional. It may be questioned, however, whether Aristotle intended it as proof and, furthermore, whether it is necessary to prove the conventionality of names. The alternatives are that names are either entirely arbitrary or conventional or natural. Socrates, in the *Cratylus*, failed to prove that they are natural. They cannot be purely arbitrary because men in communicating understand what is said. Given (1) the experience of watching language develop, (2) the existence of synonyms, homonyms, and different languages, and (3) the abortive attempt of Socrates to prove that names are natural, the signification of names must be conventional.[48] What the natural inarticulate sounds of beasts and men reveal are not things to which they refer but states of emotion. Things cannot have names unless men agree in imposing certain names on them, and if these names are to be useful in communication, then they must be conventional not arbitrary.

In the *Rhetoric* Aristotle refers to names not only as signs or symbols but as imitations: "... for words are imitations, and the voice also which of all our parts is best adapted for imitations, was ready to hand."[49] It is surprising that Aristotle should refer to them in this way since by his theory of conventional names it seems that he has excluded any theory of imitation in names. But if one takes into consideration the context of this remark it is not necessary to interpret Aristotle here as admitting the theory of the *Cratylus*: the Platonic theory that names are imitations, that is, that they have a natural likeness to that of which they are the names. Considering the difference of the medium of language and the material of things, imitation in the sense of exact image is impossible in names.

When one considers the context of the above remark about names as imitations, he finds that Aristotle is speaking about the function of language in poetry. Any work of imitation — poetry, sculpture, art — provides a means of learning that is naturally pleasing to

[48]   *Cratylus*, 397A-425E.
[49]   *Rhetoric* III: ch. 1; 1404a21.

man.[50] Poetry imitates men in action both by action, in the case of drama, and by language which represents the thought that is the cause of the action. Unlike the other arts, poetry produces its effects through symbols alone; it employs words to call up images of the objects to be represented. Imitation, therefore, need not mean similarity such that the parts of the word imitate parts of the thing. Indeed, given the difference of the material of language and the material of things, this is impossible.[51] Men, unlike animals, have an instinct for representation or imitation. As poets represent actions in metrical and enriched diction, the philosopher attempts to represent reality in language.[52]

Aristotle's theory is that meaning is given to words by the intelligence of men; it is not a natural property of a group of letters. We have not yet said what Aristotle means by signification or meaning. One does not find only one sense of the term functioning in Aristotle's use of it. Let us examine his statements about signification of words to determine what he means by signification.

2.5.2 The Meaning of Sentences

When Aristotle claims that words or phrases signify, he means that they communicate thought or that they arrest the attention of the listener who hears at least the beginning of some communication. For Aristotle, names and phrases or sentences are not significant in exactly the same way. It is clear that both sentences and some of the parts of sentences can be said to have a meaning or to signify. Let us turn first to what he says about sentences:

---

[50] *Poetics* ch. 1: 1447a16-18; 1447b1; ch. 2: 1448a1; ch. 3: 1448b5-24; ch. 6: 1449b23; ch. 9: 1451b36-38; *Rhetoric* I: ch. 11; 1371b6.

[51] *Cratylus*, 393A-428A. Note Socrates' attempts here.

[52] It is interesting to note here that Empedocles is called a poet in a secondary sense only because of the metrical nature of his writing. A poet is a poet primarily because of the imitative nature of his work. Although Empedocles uses poetic devices in writing — metaphor and ornate language — he was not imitating men in action nor the thoughts of men causing their action. See *Poetics* ch. 1: 1447b11-22.

26   ARISTOTLE'S THEORY OF SIGNIFICATION

A sentence is a significant portion of speech, some parts of which have an independent meaning, that is to say, as an utterance, though not as the expression of any judgment.[53]

It seems that Aristotle can be interpreted in the following manner. Significant phrases whose parts may also be significant are of three kinds: (1) non-predicative phrases without a verb, such as a definition: rational animal; (2) predicative phrases such as "Cleon walks"; (3) other figures or modes of speech which have a noun and a verb but are not predications, such as prayers, commands, questions.[54] Aristotle does not give any formal consideration in his works to the third type. In each type some words which are part of the phrase may be significant by themselves apart from the sentence. Although predications and non-predicative phrases are composite sounds, they signify something one or unified. A definition is one because the combination of terms signifies and stands for one thing in the same way that a name does.[55] A predication is one because the combination of terms describes a single fact and admits of only one assertion or denial.[56]

As we have seen above, Aristotle divides sentences into predicative and non-predicative sentences. A more specific meaning of signification arises from the division:

Every sentence has meaning, not as being the natural means by which a physical faculty is realized, but, as we have said, by convention. Yet every sentence is not a proposition; only such are propositions as have in them either truth or falsity. Thus a prayer is a sentence, but is neither true or false.[57]

[53] *De Int.* ch. 4: 16b26 ff. Robins errs in saying that Aristotle defines sentence as affirming or denying a predicate of its subject. Robert Henry Robins, *Ancient and Medieval Grammatical Theory in Europe* (London: Bell, 1951), p. 21.
[54] This interpretation is gleaned from *Poetics* ch. 20: 1457a23-30; ch. 19: 1456b8-10. It is broader than Bywater's interpretation; cf. Ingram Bywater, *Aristotle on the Art of Poetry* (Oxford: At the Clarendon Press, 1909), p. 277.
[55] On the unity of definition, see *De Int.* ch. 5: 17a8; ch. 11: 21a29; *Post. An.* II: ch. 10; 93b35; *Met.* VII: ch. 4; 103b9; VIII: ch. 6; 1045a12.
[56] *De Int.* ch. 5: 17a16. Several sentences may be said to be one if joined by a conjunction, such as the *Iliad*.
[57] *De Int.* ch. 4: 17a1. Ordinarily Aristotle uses the terms κατάφασις and ἀπόφασις for affirmations and negations respectively. Occasionally he substitutes φάσις which strictly means a diction or word, for κατάφασις. Cf. Bonitz, *Index*, p. 810b7-8. Only the predication admits of judgment regarding its truth or falsity. Every enunciation is basically a predication.

The predicative sentence — the proposition or enunciation — signifies truth or falsity in contrast to non-predicative sentences — prayers, commands, questions, poetical sentences — which signify in the sense that they communicate thought but do not assert the truth or falsity of what things are. Meaning, for Aristotle, is broader than the meaning of enunciations signifying truth or falsity. But it is only the enunciation with which Aristotle is concerned in logic which is the method of science.[58] By confining his attention in logic to enunciations, Aristotle falsely suggests that there cannot be logical relations between sentences of other types. Later we will consider his reason for the restricted scope of logic. It suffices now to note that this concern with enunciations signifying truth and falsity indicates that Aristotle cannot be interested in grammar which is concerned only with the relation and order of words in sentences and not with the true and false references of enunciations. Let us turn now to the parts of sentences that have meaning.

2.5.3   *The Meaning of Parts of Sentences*

Parts of significant sentences may be divided into (1) sounds without meaning, and (2) significant sounds, the noun and the verb, these latter being the ones that signify apart from sentences. Articles, conjunctions, and distributive pronouns are meaningless sounds which do not have meaning when expressed by themselves but have a function when used with significant words. The conjunction is a meaningless sound which neither hinders nor causes the formation of a single significant sound or phrase out of several sounds and which, if the phrase stands by itself, cannot properly stand at the beginning of it, or a conjunction may be a meaningless sound which, together with meaningful words, is capable of forming one significant phrase.[59] The article is a sound without meaning which marks the beginning or end of a phrase or a division in it

---

[58]   *Ibid.*, 17a5-7; *In De Int.* less. 7, #85-87.
[59]   *Poetics* ch. 20: 1456b38-1457a5.

and naturally stands at either end or in the middle of the sentence.⁶⁰
The distributive pronoun, used with a noun, indicates whether a
name is taken universally or not.⁶¹

A problem arises here which Aristotle does not mention. The
sounds of brute animals are also called by Aristotle meaningless
sounds (φωνή). Yet the syncategorematic words, as the conjunction, article and distributive pronoun are later called, are not the
same as brute sounds. What differentiates them evidently, must
be articulation by the tongue and lips as well as the conventional
use of them with significant words.⁶² While they are not names,
in the strict sense, as we shall see, they are *words* distinct from the
meaningless natural sounds of men and beasts which are not even
words. One can see more clearly here how the words that are called
meaningless sounds can be said to signify in a secondary sense. The
sounds of brutes in conjunction with meaningful sounds do not
have a function in a sentence, whereas the article, conjunction, and
pronoun do have a function.

2.5.3.1 *The Noun*

As for the meaningful parts of sentences, are the noun and the
verb the only parts that are meaningful? Although these are the
only meaningful parts treated in *De Interpretatione*, in the *Categories* Aristotle refers to more than the grammatical noun and verb
as significant: "Expressions which are in no way composite signify
substance, quantity, quality, relation, place, time, position, state,

---

⁶⁰ *Ibid.*, 1457a5-10.
⁶¹ *De Int.* ch. 10: 20a7-15. Aristotle limits sounds with meaning to nouns and
verbs; yet he speaks here of pronouns as signifying (σημαίνει) that something
is taken universally. This, then, is another meaning of signification: a word
that by itself is meaningless can when taken with a name signify the extension
of that name. In this way also, it seems that articles and conjunctions, in their
functions, may be said to have signification.
⁶² *Hist. An.* IV: ch. 9; 535a27 ff; *Poetics* ch. 20: 1456b22-25. A letter is not
any sound without meaning but one from which an intelligible sound can be
formed. Sounds of animals are not articulated letters.

action, or affection."[63] According to this statement, the noun and the verb are not the only significant grammatical parts of a speech. Other parts of speech are significant in that they communicate thought to a listener. Let us examine Aristotle's meaning of "noun" and "verb" in order to understand how they can be the only meaningful parts of speech.

By a noun we mean a sound significant by convention, which has no reference to time, and of which no part is significant apart from the rest. In the noun 'Fairsteed', the part 'steed' has no significance in and by itself, as in the phrase 'fair steed'. Yet there is a difference between the simple and composite nouns; for in the former the part is in no way significant, in the latter it contributes to the meaning of the whole, although it has not an independent meaning. Thus in the word 'pirate-boat' the word 'boat' has no meaning except as part of the whole word.[64]

What distinguishes the noun from the sentence or phrase is that no part of it has meaning by itself. In a compound name no part retains the meaning it would have as a separate word. This points up again the conventionality of word, for no part of a word signifies a part of the thing named; any significant part of a word is not in itself significant as to the whole name. Herein a compound word differs from a phrase such as "rational animal", each part of which is significant in itself.

Aristotle broadens the meaning of "noun" to include expressions such as "non-man" because there is no other simple term to designate these indefinite nouns. These do not signify determinate natures, but can be predicated of both what does and what does not exist in reality.[65] St. Thomas explains that a noun must signify either a determinate nature, such as "man"; a determinate person such as a pronoun does; or both, as proper names do.[66] Cases or modes of nouns such as "of Philo" are not nouns in the strict sense;

[63]   *Cat.* ch. 4: 1b25.
[64]   *De Int.* ch. 2: 16a19-27. Cf. *Poetics* ch. 21: 1457a11-14, a33. "Name" would be a better translation of ὄνομα than "noun" because, as we shall see, "name" will be a generic term covering both the name in the strict sense and verb. Cf. *infra* pp. 32-33
[65]   *Ibid.*, 16a32-33.
[66]   *In De Int.*, less. 4; #48. This apparently justifies Aristotle's use of a proper name as an example of a name; Cf. Ackrill, *op. cit.*, p. 115. Proper names also fulfill Aristotle's definition of noun in the strict sense insofar as when coupled with a verb they can signify truth or falsity.

although the definition of "noun" may be applied to them, they fall short of being nouns since when coupled with a verb they do not signify truth or falsity. When Aristotle says the definition of "noun" may be applied to them, he seems to mean that they are significant but since the nominative is first a noun, the definition of "noun" may be applied to the oblique cases only secondarily.[67] This criterion regarding the primary use of "noun" indicates that Aristotle is interested in nouns logically, as they are subjects of enunciations.

To summarize, a noun strictly speaking is a significant sound communicating thought without expressing time; no part of the noun is significant apart from the rest of the word. When coupled with a verb it signifies truth and falsity. More broadly, the noun includes (1) indefinite nouns such as "non-man"; (2) oblique cases of nouns such as "of Philo". Aristotle defines "noun" specifically not as a grammatical part of speech but as a logical one, according to its ability to function as the subject of an enunciation.

2.5.3.2 The Verb

As for the verb, Aristotle defines it by differentiating it from the noun and the sentence:

A verb is that which, in addition to its proper meaning, carries with it the notion of time. No part of it has any independent meaning, and it is a sign of something said of something else; ... i.e. of something either predicable of or present in some other thing.[68]

The first element of the verb, its signification with time, differentiates it from the noun; since no part of it has an independent meaning it is different also from the sentence; as a sign of something said of something else, it is differentiated from the noun and from the participle which also signifies with time.[69] Which of these three

---

[67] *Ibid.*, #49.
[68] *De Int.* ch. 3: 16b6-8, 11.
[69] *In De Int.*, less. 5; #55. The definition of the verb in the *Poetics* omits the note of a verb whereby it is a sign of something said of something else. "A verb is a composite sound with a meaning, indicative of time, no part of which has a meaning by itself — just as in nouns." ch. 20: 1457a14-15.

elements is the formal note of the verb? St. Thomas seems to hold the view that the verb's being a sign of something said of something else is its formal note.[70] He notes the disjunction used by Aristotle, "something belonging to a subject *or* in a subject" refers to both essential and accidental predication. Although a verb is always a sign of those things that are predicated of another, it is not always the thing signified by the verb that is predicated. In the case of essential predication, it is a noun that is predicated, e.g., "Man is animal". According to St. Thomas, predication pertains more properly to composition:

For predication seems to pertain more properly to composition; therefore, the verbs themselves are what are predicated, rather than signify predicates. The verb is a sign that something is being predicated because all predication is made through the verb by reason of the composition introduced, whether what is being predicated is predicated essentially or accidentally.[71]

Taken by itself, a verb may be called a name or noun (ὄνομα);

Verbs in and by themselves are substantival and have significance, for he who uses such expressions arrests the hearer's mind, and fixes his attention; but they do not, as they stand, express any judgment, either positive or negative.[72]

According to Gilson, in this passage Aristotle is reducing the verb to a noun.[73] Gilson does not notice that Aristotle is distinguishing the verb in a proposition and the verb taken by itself absolutely. For Aristotle, according to Gilson, verbs are names which do not signify accomplished action, or the states which result from action; they signify the concepts corresponding to these actions.[74] But in the passage quoted, Aristotle is giving us a broader meaning of name and the broad grammatical meaning of verb. Generally, a name is what signifies in and by itself, including both grammatical nouns and verbs; more strictly it means the significant noun as

---

[70]   *Ibid.*, #59-61. Others hold that to signify action or with time is the formal note of the verb. See opinions in Emmanuel Trépanier, "Philosophes et grammariens sur la définition du verbe", *Laval Théologique et Philosophique*, XVII (1961), 87-99. Trépanier agrees with St. Thomas.

[71]   *In De Int.*, less. 5; #60.

[72]   *De Int.* ch. 3; 16b19-22. Words in general are called names in *Poetics* ch. 20: 1457a10; ch. 21: 1457b25; ch. 22: 1458b20; ch. 25: 1461a31.

[73]   Etienne Gilson, *L'Être et l'essence* (Paris: Librairie Philosophique J. Vrin, 1948), pp. 272-275.

[74]   *Ibid.*, p. 273.

distinct from the verb which when coupled with a verb signifies truth or falsity. The verb is properly a verb only when predicated of a subject in a proposition. Aristotle does not here explicitly distinguish the non-predicative sentence from the proposition which he defines as signifying truth or falsity. But according as he has distinguished the different kinds of sentences, only a predication such as "Cleon walks" admits of a judgment of truth or falsity. Every judgment is, basically, a predication.

Just as in the case of nouns, for want of a proper name, Aristotle calls expressions such as "is not-healthy" indefinite verbs since they apply equally to being and to non-being. Since the verb indicates present time, the tenses of verbs are verbs only secondarily. The verb, most properly, is a sign of composition in predication. Taken by itself, outside a proposition, it may be called a name since it signifies in the same way a name does. Indefinite verbs and tenses of verbs other than the present may be called verbs in a secondary sense. It is clear, then, that Aristotle defines "verb" primarily in terms not of its grammatical function but of its logical function — predication in an enunciation.

Regarding the other grammatical parts of speech, Bywater finds that for Aristotle the term name (ὄνομα) must be taken to include not only nouns, but also adjectives, personal and demonstrative pronouns, and possibly even the article as a kind of pronoun — in fact all the declinable parts of speech except perhaps the relatives, which may have been classed among the conjunctions.[75] Perhaps the reason for this is that "case" as used by Aristotle is broader than the present grammatical usage. Besides (1) tense, number, and voice of verbs, and the genders and cases of nouns, "case" includes (2) the adjectives derived from the noun and the adverb derived from the adjective as well as (3) the singular and plural forms of nouns. The adjectives and adverbs are reduced to the noun and the verb.[76] When Aristotle says, therefore, that

---

[75]   Bywater, *op. cit.*, p. 274.
[76]   *Ibid.*, pp. 262, 275; *Poetics* ch. 20: 1457a18; 1456b20; Theodorus Waitz, *Aristotelis Organon Graece*, I (Lipsiae: Sumtibus Hahnii, 1844), pp. 328-329. *De Int.* ch. 1: 16b1.

"Expressions ... signify substance, quantity, quality, ..." he is reducing these expressions to nouns and verbs in the broad sense including their cases. It is Aristotle's interest that guides his definition of "case". The inclusion of the singular and plural nominatives as cases of names indicates that case is a logical distinction at least in this context and that the definitions of noun and verb are logical, geared to a logic of general names.

2.5.3.3 *Summary*

By the convention of men certain groups of letters have the property of significance. Sentences and phrases as well as some parts of sentences have meaning in that they arrest the attention of the listener by communicating an expression that can be understood.

In asserting truth or falsity, or in asking, commanding or advising, sentences have meaning. Aristotle focuses on a second meaning of significance as a property of enunciations that express truth or falsity. This is the relevant sense of meaning in logic for Aristotle who defines the verb strictly according as it is a sign of composition in predication and the noun as a subject coupled with a verb. The logic of enunciation is not directly concerned with the other parts of speech — meaningless words — that have been distinguished by Aristotle: the article, the conjunction, the pronoun.

Yet in a third sense the meaningless words may be said to "signify" since they have a function when used with significant words. By themselves they do not name any of the things included in the categories but together with category words they have a meaning.

In summary, we see that Aristotle refers to whatever arrests the attention by communicating an understanding as "significant". Logical significance, however, at least in this context, refers to (1) sentences which are enunciations and (2) nouns and verbs according as they are the subjects and predicates of these enunciations. Meaning in philosophy will receive further specification when we examine Aristotle's concept of philosophy or scientific knowledge.

2.6 REFERENCE

We have seen that meaning, for Aristotle, is a property whereby words or combinations of words arrest the attention by communicating an expression that can be understood. Words, however, do not merely generate understanding in the mind of another person; they refer beyond themselves so that not only can a sentence be translated but what it refers to outside of language can be understood. Aristotle refers words to things through thought; thus he has a triadic theory of signification: the word is a symbol of a thought which is a likeness of the thing signified. Because the intellect is not limited to a single grasp of an individual, it can impose as many names as there are different grasps of things, and even many names or synonyms for the same thing. Thus Callias may be understood as man, as father, as animal, as white, all of which are true of him.

What are the things to which words refer for Aristotle? There is, first, the individual named by a proper name as distinct from other individuals: "Callias", "Socrates", and so forth. There is also the nature that individuals have in common with other individuals; thus we have names that signify these natures: "Man", "dog", "horse". Attributes of individuals or of natures are signified by such words as "white", "rational", "dark", "biped".

Things as known are also named by the human intellect. Aristotle has, therefore, words that refer to or signify these names: "noun", "verb", "article", "univocal", "equivocal", "metaphor". The referent of such names is directly language and indirectly the thing named. Fifthly, concepts of things or things as known are related by the intellect. Such relations are referred to by "genus", "species", "difference", "subject", "predicate".

There are also mental accidents to which words like "concept", "thought", "percept" refer. Lastly, there are fictitious entities; these names are those with which the writer of fables, the poet, and the mythologist are concerned.

We see, then, that the "things of which our experiences are the images" or the "things" to which our words refer may be individuals, nature, attributes of these, names themselves, relations of our concepts of things, mental accidents, and fictitious entities. "Thing" used here as the term of reference is used very broadly and does not mean an object. Hence the reference of what Aristotle calls "names" (either in the broad sense of verbs, nouns and their cases or in the narrower sense of the noun) is not denotation in the modern sense. Aristotle does not imply that all sorts of abstract entities and fictional entities have objective existence.

Later we shall determine which names are relevant for the philosopher who wants to obtain knowledge of reality. Let us first turn to the question of whether Aristotle was concerned with grammar.

2.7 LANGUAGE: GRAMMAR OR LOGIC?

At the beginning of this work, we claimed that Aristotle, in his use of language in philosophy, intends to talk about reality as distinct from language. If so, then his interest in language cannot be merely a grammatical one. He cannot be interested in the rules of communication, the fulfillment of which should enable men to understand each other in speaking. Before examining the possibilities of Aristotle's being a grammarian, let us determine what we mean by the term grammar.

There is a sense in which to ask whether Aristotle is a grammarian is an anachronistic question. The term *grammata* at the time of Aristotle meant "letters of the alphabet"; *grammaticus* indicated simply a person of ordinary education who was able to read and write.[77] No formal science of grammar had yet been established. Protogoras of Abdera had distinguished moods — question and answer, prayer and command — as well as the genders;[78] Prodicus of Ceos had written a treatise on synonyms; Plato had recognized two distinct parts of speech: the noun and verb. As we have said, at the time of Plato the study of the art of writing had taken the turn to the study of letters as elements of words and their phonetic

---

[77] *Topics* V: ch. 5; 142b31 ff; John Edwin Sandys, *A History of Classical Scholarship*, I (Cambridge: At the University Press, 1908-1921), 6.
[78] *Rhetoric* III: ch. 5; 1407b7; *Sophistical Refutations*, ch. 14.

value, as well as the more important problem of the relation of these sounds to thought and reality, i.e. why a certain combination of letters is the representation of one idea while another combination represents a different idea.[79] Robins tells us that

> ... grammatical study begins whenever in the stream of speech or the expanse of writing there are observed, and in some way systematized, similarities of form or patterns of arrangement, and these are partly at least correlated with the meaning or functions of the utterances in which they occur.[80]

Although grammatical distinctions had been made prior to the time of Aristotle and were used by Aristotle, they had not been made as part of the formal science of grammar. The first formal treatise of grammar was *Techné Grammatiké* of Dionysius Thrax in the first century before Christ.

In asking whether Aristotle's interest in language is a grammatical one, we are asking whether his interest was one of formulating the rules of speech in general. Perhaps now it is proper to frame the question in this manner: Are the considerations of language which are involved in doing philosophy grammatical ones? Or is philosophy itself a grammatical enterprise? Thus far, several things we have noted incline us to the view that Aristotle did intend to speak about reality and not just about language. First, his own words indicate that he is interested, as his predecessors were, in the causes of all things. Secondly, his theory of conventional signification, referring words to things through thought, indicates that he is interested in what is expressed and not merely in the conventional rules of clear and correct speech. Words are spoken not only to someone; they are spoken about something.

The formal statements of Aristotle about language do not indicate that his interest in language is grammatical. His consideration of language in the *De Interpretatione* is ordered to logic as an instrument for arguing about the natures and attributes of real things. Besides using the *De Interpretatione*, we have depended in part,

---

[79] *Cratylus*, 285C-D; *Sophist* 253A. For Aristotle with his theory of conventionality of names, the problem of the relation of sound to thought or things ceased to be a problem.
[80] Robert Henry Robins, *Ancient and Medieval Grammatical Theory in Europe* (London: Bell, 1951), p. 14.

on the formal statements regarding language in Aristotle's *Poetics* and *Rhetoric*. As we have noted, the verb in the *Poetics* is defined as "a composite sound with a meaning, indicative of time, no part of which has a meaning by itself..."[81] This definition lacks the mark of the logical verb, "a sign of something said of something else". This grammatical definition of the verb in the *Poetics* leads us to ask whether Aristotle's interest in language there is one of a grammarian. Let us examine the *Poetics* and the *Rhetoric* for indications of this.

Grammatical considerations may be identified both in the *Poetics* and the *Rhetoric* as the pure and correct Greek that is basic to the particular style of poetry or of prose.[82] Aristotle does not elaborate nor comment on the rules of pure and correct Greek. In the *Rhetoric* III, chapter five, he describes pure language as that which is opposed to solecism and barbarism and all impropriety in general. He reduces this impropriety to five rules in which purity of idiom is not distinguished from perspicuity achieved by punctuation and parenthesis.[83] Apart from this Aristotle assumes that the rules of correct Greek are understood. It is possible that grammatical matters could include the particular stylistic questions of poetry and prose treated in these two works, but such style is proper only to poetry or rhetoric and not to language in general. Furthermore, in both rhetoric and poetry, as Aristotle sees them, it is the arguments about things that are the chief elements to which the consideration of diction and language is ordered:

The poet is not a poet in so far as he merely clothes a traditional story in new verses. He is required to *make* something for himself, namely that structure of events in which universals may come to expression; ... What the poet 'makes', then, is not the actuality of events but their logical structure, their meaning.[84]

In the *Rhetoric* Aristotle apologizes for including a treatment of style:

[81] Ch. 20: 1457a14.
[82] *Rhet.* III: ch. 5.
[83] Cf. Edward Meredith Cope, *The Rhetoric of Aristotle with a Commentary*, ed. John Edwin Sandys, III (Cambridge: At the University Press, 1877), pp. 54-55.
[84] Gerald F. Else, *Aristotle's Poetics: The Argument* (Cambridge: Harvard University Press, 1957), pp. 320-321.

For justice should consist in fighting the case with the facts alone, so that everything else that is beside demonstration is superfluous; nevertheless, as we have
just said, it is of great importance owing to the corruption of the hearer. However, in every system of instruction there is some slight necessity to pay attention
to style; for it does make a difference, for the purpose of making a thing clear,
to speak in this or that manner; still, the difference is not so very great, but all
these things are mere outward show for pleasing the hearer; wherefore no one
teaches geometry in this way.[85]

Diction and style are important elements of both poetry and prose
because not only are the arguments — the *mythos* or plot in poetry
and the examples and enthymemes in rhetoric — expressed in language, but in addition to these arguments both poetry and rhetoric
make use of enriched and ornamental language in representing
action and in conveying the speaker's feeling or appealing to the
emotions of an audience. It is, in the case of rhetoric, the intellec-
tually unenlightened condition of the audience that allows the
orator to depart from scientific or logical proofs proper to the
subject matter and to make direct appeal to the feelings of the
audience.[86] The manner of expression, however, is always secondary to the arguments.

A brief examination of the grammatical distinctions of the *Poetics*
will indicate that the book is not concerned with grammar in general. Aristotle refers the student of rhetoric to the *Poetics* for a general treatment of grammatical distinctions and style.[87] The principles
of grammar treated in the *Poetics* are (1) figures of speech, (2) parts
of speech, and (3) poetic style or the selections of words and con-
structions proper to poetry.[88] Since the matter of figures of speech
belongs properly to rhetoric, Aristotle does not treat it in detail in
the *Poetics*.[89]

The parts of speech enumerated and explained in chapter twenty
of the *Poetics* involve a wider division than that of present grammar.
This division includes (1) elements into which words can be ana-

[85]   *Rhet.* III: ch. 1; 1404a4-12.
[86]   *Ibid.*, I: ch. 1; 1354a11; III: ch. 1, 1404a4-12.
[87]   *Ibid.*, III: ch. 1; 1404a39; 1404b7.
[88]   Bywater, *op. cit.*, p. 259. *Poetics* ch. 19: 1456b13.
[89]   *Poetics* ch. 19: 1456b19. Apparently it is the *Rhetoric* to which Aristotle
refers.

lyzed: the element and the syllable; (2) the various kinds of words: noun, verb, articles, conjunction and case; (3) the sentence or phrase.[90] Chapter twenty-one enumerates the kinds of nouns — simple and compound — and the properties of nouns leading to a consideration of the kinds of words proper to poetic style in chapter twenty-two. It is important to note that the grammatical distinctions made in chapter twenty serve simply as basic definitions for the treatment of poetic style in subsequent chapters. The grammatical distinctions, then, are ordered not to more complex grammatical rules but to style, a matter which in poetry and rhetoric is secondary to the arguments.

In the *Rhetoric* Aristotle's treatment of diction and style is found in Book III. Assuming the grammatical principles enumerated in the *Poetics*, he devotes the first twelve chapters of Book III to the choice of words and style proper to the orator, for knowing how to say something makes speech appear to be of a certain character.[91] For the sake of clarity, the matter of style must be attended to in every system of instruction, particularly in that system which employs rhetoric dependent for its effects not simply on the arguments but on the manner of expression. But here, also, "justice should consist in fighting the case with the facts alone".

At the beginning of this section, we asked whether the works in which Aristotle makes formal statements about language indicate that his interest in language is a grammatical one. The fact that the *De Interpretatione* is concerned with the elements only of enunciations indicates that it is not a work of general grammar; it reveals that Aristotle's interest in language is logical rather than grammatical. The *Rhetoric* and *Poetics* are chiefly concerned with arguments — enthymemes and examples in the former and the structure of the plot in the latter. The question of language is important in these works because both retoric and poetry make use of enriched and ornamental language in representing action and in conveying the speaker's feeling or appealing to emotions of the audience. The

---

[90]   Ch. 19, 20.
[91]   *Rhet*. III: ch. 1; 1403b16-17.

differences in the treatment of the parts of speech in each work seem to depend on the differences in speech according as it serves the end of logical demonstration, poetical construction and rhetorical persuasion respectively. Grammatical topics seem to be basic to questions of style and method proper to each art, but Aristotle makes no positive and detailed elaboration of pure and correct Greek.

Because a science of grammar had not yet been fully developed, a clear distinction between logic and grammar had not yet been made; at the time Aristotle wrote some distinction had been made between (1) the knowledge of reading and writing in general, (2) the stylistic points of poetry and rhetoric, and (3) logic. Even when logic and grammar have been clearly distinguished, logic will always presuppose a correct use of grammar but logic does not indicate what correct grammatical usage is. Inasmuch as Aristotle was doing logic, it was necessary for him to use at least some of the existing grammatical distinctions necessary for the expression of language. This is not to say, of course, that Aristotle did not influence in any way the development of grammar.[92]

2.8 SIGNIFICATION OF GENERAL TERMS

We have seen that Aristotle's theory of signification indicates that words point beyond themselves through thought to things. Yet not all words or sentences pointing beyond themselves have the same degree of relevance for philosophy. Perhaps it would be well to say something about what philosophy is before turning to the kinds of words and sentences that are relevant for it.

Negatively, philosophy is not history whose judgments are about singular past events; it is not poetry whose judgments are about what is possible as being probable or necessary. But the judgments of philosophy are more like those of poetry which are of the nature of universals.[93] Poetry and philosophy differ, however, in regard

---

[92] Robins, *op. cit.*, p. 24 for Aristotle's influence on grammar.
[93] *Poetics* ch. 9: 1451a36-b8.

to the language in which each expresses its truths; the poet uses language enriched with meter, harmony, and foreign words;[94] for the serious study of any subject, including philosophy, no one uses fine language.[95] Philosophy differs from poetry, also in that it is concerned with the causes and principles of real things whereas the poet must create or make his characters and his plots. When we say that philosophy is about real things we mean that even at the starting point of his inquiry, the philosopher must know that his subject exists and have some knowledge of what it is.

The pre-existent knowledge required is of two kinds. In some cases admission of the fact must be assumed, in others comprehension of the meaning of the term used, and sometimes both assumptions are essential...[96]

It is evident, for example, according to the meaning of "nature" that we are naming something that exists; to attempt to prove its existence is absurd.[97]

Besides differing from poetry and history, speculative philosophy is distinct from productive and practical sciences; it is theoretical, pursued for its own sake. Originating out of the wonder of men about small difficulties, philosophy brings one to the state of dispelled ignorance even about matters of great consequence.[98] Aristotle speaks about this terminal state of wisdom which the philosopher reaches as scientific knowledge. But what is the meaning of knowledge that is scientific?

It is not knowledge of the particular obtained through perception. Rather scientific knowledge involves the knowledge of the universal:

Scientific knowledge is not possible through the act of perception... for perception must be of a particular, whereas scientific knowledge involves the recognition of the commensurate universal.[99]

[94] *Ibid.*, ch. 6: 1449b25.
[95] *Rhet.* III: ch. 1; 1404a5-12.
[96] *Post. An.* I: ch. 1; 71a11-12.
[97] "That nature exists, it would be absurd to try to prove; for it is obvious that there are many things of this kind, and to prove what is obvious by what is not is the mark of a man who is unable to distinguish what is self-evident from what is not." *Physics* II: ch. 1; 193a1-6.
[98] *Met.* I: ch. 2; 982b20.
[99] *Post. An.* I: ch. 31; 87b27; 38-39; ch. 33. *Nich. Eth.* VI: ch. 6; 1140b31-32.

For this reason Aristotle frames such general or universal problems as "We must clearly acquire knowledge of factors that are primary".[100]

One may ask, now, what is the process by which one arrives at these universals? By the power known as intuitive reason, Aristotle explains, the mind after experience of a certain number of particular instances, grasps a universal truth.[101] The passage from particular to universal is made possible by the fact that perception itself has an element of the universal in that what is perceived in a particular thing is the character which it shares with other things. For example, the perception of one man, while we still remember perceiving another, leads to the grasping of universal man:

When one of a number of logically indiscriminable particulars has made a stand, the earliest universal is present in the soul: for though the act of sense-perception is of the particular, its content is universal — is man, for example, not the man Callias. A fresh stand is made among these rudimentary universals, and the process does not cease until the indivisible concepts, the true universals, are established: e.g. such and such a species of animal is a step towards the genus animal, which by the same process is a step towards a further generalization.[102]

In this way the mind passes to the highest universals of all — the categories which cannot be analyzed into genus and difference.[103]

Aristotle, however, does not accept all of these universals as subjects of science. As a rule, arguments and inquiries are concerned with predicates which are predicated of others and about which predication can be made.[104]

---

[100] *Met.* I: ch. 3; 983a23 ff.
[101] *Nich. Eth.* VI: ch. 6; 1140b31-1141a8; VI: ch. 7; 1141a16-19; ch. 3; 1139b27-34.
[102] *Post. An.* II: ch. 19; 100a14-b4.
[103] The question at hand, in this chapter, is how we know the first principles of science. Aristotle argues that just as we reach universal concepts by induction from sense perception, so we come to know the first principles of science.
[104] "Of these ultimate predicates, it is not possible to demonstrate another predicate, save as a matter of opinion (κατὰ δόξαν), but these may be predicated of other things. Neither can individuals be predicated of other things, though other things can be predicated of them. Whatever lies between these limits can be spoken of in both ways: they may be stated of others, and others stated of them. And as a rule arguments and inquiries are concerned with these things." *Prior An.* I: ch. 27; 43a36-43. This, of course, affects the possibility of being *qua* being as the subject of metaphysics. Tricot notes that κατὰ δόξαν is synonymous with διαλεκτικῶς; nothing is so general that one cannot attribute

If the subject of science is universal, being particular only insofar as the particular is included in the universal, logic or the method
of philosophy is developed for a science that uses universal terms
and statements. One may ask, then, to what do these general terms
refer? Do they signify real things? The universal is symbolized
by a simple expression, in the way in which the highest universals
— the categories — are expressed in language by a diction or
φάσις. Although the terms symbolize the universal in the mind,
that universal has been apprehended from things. The universals
exist in the individuals.

We see that philosophy or scientific knowledge in Aristotle's
sense will have no problem about the unique reference of its terms.
Because of what Aristotle means by philosophy and scientific
knowledge, a term is never ambiguous in the sense of not having
a unique reference but can be ambiguous only if it is a term whose
meaning is not definite, as we shall see. The terms symbolizing
immediately the universal in the mind, refer indirectly to the common characteristics in any individuals having those characteristics.
Thus Aristotle can say, "By 'having a meaning' I mean this: if
'man' is 'two-footed animal', then if anything is a man, its 'being-
two-footed' will be what its 'being-a-man' is".[105] General terms
are of particular importance in philosophy. While referring directly to the universal as grasped by the mind, they still refer ultimately
to real things.

2.9 CONCLUSION

In summary, then, we have seen that Aristotle does not explicitly
specify different meanings of "meaning" or "signification" corresponding to the different uses of language. But it is just this that
can be done on the basis of what we have seen in this chapter. If
one were to ask what is philosophical meaning for Aristotle, it

---

to it something the same in kind as "Being is one". J. Tricot, *Organon* III:
Les premiers analytiques (Paris: Librairie Philosophique J. Vrin, 1936), p. 137,
n. 2.
[105]   *Met.* IV: ch. 4; 1006a31-33.

would not be difficult to see that philosophical meaning depends on the meaning of philosophy. For Aristotle, philosophy is science of the real; therefore language in philosophy will refer to things outside the mind. The reference is not the denotation of objects. Words refer to the concept in the mind which may be the concept of an individual object, a universal nature, attributes of these, names themselves, relations of our concepts of things, mental accidents, or fictitious entities. Because the language used in philosophy refers to reality, philosophy will not be simply a grammatical clarification of language. We will show more arguments for this conclusion; for now it is evident that the three works — *De Interpretatione*, *Poetics*, and *Rhetoric* — do not display a grammatical concern with language but rather are concerned primarily with arguments about things and with the style proper to poetry and oratory.

Secondly we noted that because philosophy is interested in the attributes and properties of a subject, its language will involve only those sentences which enunciate a predicate of a subject. We see thus far that philosophical meaning will differ from meaning in general because of the kinds of statements that will be significant in speculative philosophy and the nature of the referents of those statements. It remains now to attempt to explain Aristotle's statement that philosophical language is the language of proof.

PHILOSOPHICAL LANGUAGE

3.1 INTRODUCTION

We have seen in the previous chapter how, for Aristotle, words signify and in particular how the general terms of philosophy can signify. Aristotle, however, requires further precision of language for those who would speak meaningfully about reality and its causes. Although he has no one work devoted to the language of philosophy, Aristotle has much to say in various places about what it is. In this chapter we will attempt to glean the meaning of philosophical language from Aristotle's writings.

In the *Metaphysics*[1] Aristotle, without elaboration, identifies the language of philosophers as the "language of proof". The first task in this chapter is to determine what is the meaning of "language of proof". What kinds of proofs does Aristotle admit in philosophy and why? The next task is to determine what restrictions he places on the language used in these proofs. We can rely on some formal statements of Aristotle for these restrictions, and his recommendations with regard to clarity of language are exemplified in the criticism of his predecessors. The restrictions Aristotle places on language raise the question whether terminology in philosophy is restricted to the use of univocal terms. The last part of this chapter will be concerned with the solution to this question.

---

[1] III: ch. 4; 1000a18-22.

3.1.1   *The Problem*

Aristotle's general criterion for philosophical language according
to which he recognizes his predecessors from Thales to Plato as
philosophers, is the use of the language of proof (ἀπόδειξις). He
opposes this kind of language to the spurious wisdom of myths
"that make no sense to us". Aristotle, however, does not elucidate
the meaning of "language of proof". In an attempt to understand
what he means by this expression, we shall examine the context
in which he uses it.

3.1.2   *Hesiod and Empedocles*

Aristotle uses the expression in the course of his aporematic treatment of the question "whether perishable and imperishable things
have the same or different principles".[2] The curious thing is that
while neither Hesiod nor Empedocles answers this question satis-
factorily, Aristotle, on the basis of their answers, rejects Hesiod
as a philosopher but accepts Empedocles as one, "But why should
we examine seriously the spurious wisdom of myths? We must
look for information to those who use the language of demonstration ..."[3] and then turns to Empedocles for an explanation. What
is the reason for the difference in Aristotle's attitude to these two
answers? Let us examine them in order to determine this.

Hesiod and the theologians present the principles as gods; those
of the gods who did not taste nectar and ambrosia were made
mortal; those who did were immortal. Aristotle criticizes this explanation as using words — nectar and ambrosia — that are significant only to Hesiod and the theologians. Hesiod then is not
using terms that provide a commonly understood explanation.
"Nectar and ambrosia" refer to a kind of food but, according to
Aristotle, it is impossible that being eternal should depend on a
type of food, for one takes food either for the sake of pleasure or
for sustenance:

---

[2]   *Met.* III: ch. 4; 1000a10.
[3]   *Met.* III: ch. 4; 1000a18-21.

If the gods take nectar and ambrosia for the sake of pleasure, their doing so does not explain their being; and if the gods do so for the sake of their very being, how could beings who need nourishment be eternal?[4]

St. Thomas indicates that some truth is hidden under this fable. It is possible that nectar and ambrosia may be understood as the supreme goodness of the First Principle. By participation of the highest goodness, some beings are rendered incorruptible. Those at a greater distance from the first principles cannot conserve their eternity.[5] If something like this is the explanation truly intended by Hesiod, then it is easy to see that the words, as Aristotle claims, are significant only to those who have written them. What drinking nectar and ambrosia are intended to refer to is in no way evident to the ordinary reader.

On the other hand, Empedocles, whom one could expect to speak consistently, does not give an account that can be correct. Yet Aristotle has referred to him as one of those who use the "language of proof". Let us examine Empedocles' solution.

Empedocles posits strife as the cause of destruction and corruption, and love as the cause of generation. Aristotle argues that since all things except God, according to Empedocles, proceed from strife — the separation of the original unity — it is impossible that strife, the cause of the generation of particular things by their separation from the original unity, be the cause of the corruption of things as well. In the same way, love cannot be the cause only of generation because when all the elements are again united by love or friendship, the world of individual things will be corrupted. Another inconsistency in Empedocles' argument is that if God is not made up of strife then he cannot know all other things consisting of friendship and strife, for, according to Empedocles' theory of knowledge, like is known by like. Again, Empedocles shows no cause of the necessity for the transposition from love to hate. While inconsistencies do appear in the argument of Empedocles, Aristotle does refer to him as using the language of proof; it is for this reason that his arguments are worthy of consideration.

[4]   *Met.* III: ch. 4; 1000a14-19.
[5]   *In. Met.* III: less. 11; #468-9.

What is the difference, then, between these two explanations of Hesiod and Empedocles? The term of explanation used by Hesiod is a phrase — drinking of nectar and ambrosia — whose referent, a fictional element, has not the power of communicating eternal being. Food has the power of giving pleasure and of sustaining life for a certain length of time, but food cannot be what Hesiod is literally referring to as the source of eternal life. What Hesiod is presenting to his reader is a story or myth. "Fables are suitable for public speaking, and they have this advantage that ... it is easier to invent fables; for they must be invented like comparisons, if a man is capable of seizing the analogy."[6]

Empedocles, on the other hand, has an argument for positing strife and friendship as causes of generation and destruction. One might say that he is drawing an analogy between the universe as a whole and man. Friendship is a principle of unity among men; strife is a principle of corruption. So, too, in the universe, love must be the principle of unity, strife of corruption. So, too, in the universe, love must be the principle of unity, strife of corruption. What Empedocles intends is the literal meaning of these terms, love and strife.[7] It may also be argued that Empedocles is not drawing an analogy but rather that he had made no distinction between the world and man. If *physis* or nature is the first metaphysical element, a substance out of which everything has taken shape, and this it is for the ancients, then one explanation of unity and disunity will hold for the universe, the gods and men.[8] The causes of the unity and disunity among men, being more evident, are seen as the causes of the unity and disunity of all things. The problem with Empedocles' argument is not that his words have no real referents, but that his argument is not consistent in itself, or with his theory of knowledge. The subtleties of the mythologists

---

[6] *Rhet.* II: ch. 20; 1394a2-5.

[7] G. S. Kirk and J. E. Raven, *The Presocratic Philosophers* (Cambridge: At the University Press, 1957), p. 330: "Empedocles believes, as the analogy shows, that sexual love and cosmic Love are one and the same self-existent eternal force which acts upon the person or thing that loves."

[8] F. M. Cornford, *From Religion to Philosophy: A Study in the Origins of Western Speculation* (New York: Harper & Bros., 1957), p. 123.

employ words that cannot be taken literally, for their referents as explanatory principles make no sense to man; while Empedocles intends the literal meaning of his words, either his analogy is incorrect or he has failed to note a necessary distinction between the universe and man. In addition to this his arguments are inconsistent and incomplete.

It is the use of a proof that seems basically to differentiate Empedocles from Hesiod. What does this mean in terms of language? The language of Hesiod is the language of myth or fables whose referents are not real things providing a true explanation. The language of proof refers to real principles of explanation, in this case love and strife. The language of proof, then, must refer to real principles and causes, not the fictional elements of the theologians and mythologists. Empedocles fulfills this criterion but his language of proof, using in this instance either a metaphor or a term with a confused meaning, still does not satisfy Aristotle's criterion for philosophical language.

What further specifications does Aristotle give for language in philosophical proofs? Before turning directly to this question, let us examine first what Aristotle means by proof and which proofs are admitted in philosophy. Then we can question whether he makes any specifications regarding language used in these proofs.

3.2 THE LANGUAGE OF PROOF

The term that Aristotle uses to mean "proof" in the phrase "language of proof" is ἀπόδειξις. In its strict sense it means exact scientific demonstration by syllogism, leading from universal and necessary truths to universal and necessary conclusions:[9]

By demonstration (ἀπόδειξιν) I mean a syllogism which produces scientific knowledge (ἐπιστήμη), in other words one which enables us to know by the mere fact that we grasp it.[10]

[9] *Post. An.* I: ch. 2; 71b18-89.
[10] "Since the object of scientific knowledge in the absolute sense cannot be otherwise than it is, the notion reached by demonstrative knowledge will be necessarily true. Now knowledge is demonstrative when we possess it in virtue of having a demonstration; therefore the premises from which demonstration is inferred are necessarily true."

But Aristotle uses ἀπόδειξις in a broader sense so that it refers to more than simply demonstrative proofs. We will indicate these broader uses of the term in order to know what possibly Aristotle may mean by the "language of proof".

3.2.1 *Proofs*

Aristotle uses the term "analytical science" (ἀναλυτικῆς ἐπιστήμης), which usually refers to the product of strict demonstration, to refer also to dialectic,

> For what we have said before is true: that Rhetoric is composed of analytical science and of that branch of political science which is concerned with Ethics, and that it resembles partly Dialectic and partly sophistical arguments.[11]

Dialectic differs from demonstration in being reasoning from generally accepted opinions which commend themselves to all, or to the majority or to the wise. Dialectic then, like rhetoric, does not deal with any one class of subjects, but is of general application.[12] It is aimed at producing conviction (πίστις) but since its premisses and conclusions are never more than probable, it can only in a broad sense be said to be a proof (ἀπόδειξις), and this because a probable proof often produces a belief or conviction as strong and certain as that which follows from demonstration. It is for this reason that Aristotle often refers to dialectic as if it had the same certitude as demonstration in the strict sense.

The nature of dialectic throws light on the nature of rhetoric since for Aristotle the two are counterparts. Neither dialectic nor rhetoric have special principles but deal with every proposition presented although rhetoric is practically confined to those things about which we deliberate, i.e. in the realm of ethics and politics.[13] The object of dialectic and rhetoric alike, as we have seen, is to produce conviction, not the ἐπιστήμη of demonstration; for this purpose it is sufficient that the premisses be probable (ἔνδοξοι),

---

Post. An. I: ch. 4; 73a21-26. Cf. also *ibid.*, ch. 24; 85b42-26; *Topics* I: ch. 1; 100a27-29.
[11]   *Rhet.* I: ch. 4; 1359b9-11.
[12]   *Rhet.* I: ch. 1; 1355b17 ff.
[13]   *Rhet.* I: ch. 1; 1355b17 ff.; ch. 2; 1358a10-31; ch. 4; 1359b10-13.

likely to win acceptance. Their method, therefore, need not be a strict syllogistic one.

The modes of persuasion or the arguments of the rhetorical method are (1) the personal character of the speaker (ἦθος), (2) putting the audience into a certain frame of mind so that it feels a certain emotion (πάθος), and (3) arguments through the speech itself — logical arguments expressed in enthymemes and examples; it is these latter that Aristotle calls ἀπόδειξις. Each of these three modes is effected through language in a different way. The personal character of the speaker is not something that the orator learns in rhetoric; whatever he is, he brings with him and it will be conveyed to the audience through what he says. The production of certain emotions is effected by the character's acting and speaking naturally. But the proof of an argument produced by the speech itself must be carefully formulated in enthymemes and examples according to the techniques learned in rhetoric and logic.

The proof in rhetoric which is a sort of demonstration (ἀπόδειξις) is the enthymeme:

... but when, certain things being posited, something different results by reason of them, alongside of them, from their being true, either universally or in most cases, such a conclusion in Dialectic is called a syllogism, in Rhetoric an enthymeme.[14]

Unlike those of the strict demonstration, the premisses and conclusions of the enthymeme are never more than probable and contingent. The enthymeme also may consist of fewer premisses, one premiss being omitted.[15] It is the logician, capable of examining the matter and forms of a syllogism who will be in the highest degree a master of rhetorical argument,

if to this he adds a knowledge of the subjects with which enthymemes deal and the differences between them and logical syllogism. For in fact, the true and that which resembles it come under the purview of the same faculty, and at the same time men have a sufficient natural capacity for the truth and indeed in most cases attain to it.[16]

---

[14] *Rhet.* I: ch. 1; 1356b13-15.
[15] *Prior. An.* II: ch. 27; 70a1-6; *Rhet.* I: ch. 2; 1357a8-22.
[16] *Rhet.* I: ch. 1; 1355a12-17.

An example, also referred to as a kind of syllogism, is of two kinds: one which consists in relating things that have happened before, and another in inventing them oneself — either comparisons or fables. The example is a case of imperfect induction; the process in the proof is up and down, from the known instance to the general rule and down to the particular conclusion required. It is an argument from analogy assuming the validity of a regular induction and demonstrating a mere probability.[17]

Aristotle uses the term ἀπόδειξις to describe these proofs of rhetoric which are not strictly demonstrative:

> If it is obvious, therefore, that a system arranged according to the rules of art is only concerned with proofs (πίστις): that proof is a sort of demonstration (ἀπόδειξις), since we are most strongly convinced when we suppose anything to have been demonstrated; that rhetorical demonstration (ἀπόδεξις ῥητορική) is an enthymeme which generally speaking is the strongest of (πίστεων) rhetorical proofs: and lastly that the enthymeme is a kind of syllogism.[18]

To call these proofs ἀπόδειξις, as Aristotle does, is not to use the term in the strict sense implying universal and necessary conclusions and rigorous syllogistic method. No conclusion of rhetoric can ever attain to this. Aristotle means only that the truths must be "demonstrated" by being as consistent with sound reasoning and the rules of logic as will induce conviction in those who hear them. The use of enthymemes and examples suffices in rhetoric because this art is concerned with the contingent matter of human actions; one must also take into account the condition of the audience which is unprepared to be convinced by strictly demonstrative proofs. The aim in rhetorical argumentation is to present those arguments which will be the most convincing. The arguments must attempt demonstrative proofs; they will be accepted by the audience as demonstrative proofs although they conclude only what is probable.[19]

Perhaps it seems strange to speak of the *arguments* of poetry, but proof that something is or is not is exactly what Aristotle sees as

---

[17] Edward Meredith Cope, *An Introduction to Aristotle's Rhetoric* (London: Macmillan and Co., 1867), p. 107.
[18] *Rhet.* I: ch. 1; 1355a4; cf. also III: ch. 17; 1417b21-22; II: ch. 1; 1377b21-24; II: ch. 20; 1394a9-18.
[19] *Rhet.* III: ch. 17; 1417b21-2; I: ch. 2; 1358a1.

one of the effects to be produced by the element of thought, as opposed to character, in poetry:

> Under the head of Thought come all the effects to be produced by language. Some of these are proof and refutation (ἀποδεικνύναι), the arousing of feelings like pity, fear, anger, and so on, and then again exaggeration and depreciation.[20]

> 'Thought' you find in speeches which contain an argument (ἀποδεικνουνσί) that something is or is not, or a general expression of opinion.[21]

Aristotle does not in the *Poetics* elaborate this element of poetry because the subject is proper to rhetoric.[22] As we have seen, the production of certain emotions is effected by the character's acting naturally but the proof of an argument that something is so and so, for example, the actual argument of a case such as Hecuba's accusation of Helen before Menelaus, is produced by the speech itself and depends on the logical techniques of the rhetorician.

Which of the above mentioned proofs are useful for the purpose of speculative philosophy? The matter of proof in both rhetoric and poetry is a concern for the art of rhetoric. The rhetorical modes of persuasion arising from the personal character of the speaker and the emotional conditioning of the audience do not pertain to speculative philosophy which, unlike rhetoric, does not aim to persuade regarding the contingent matter of human actions but to attain knowledge of the causes of reality.[23] The enthymemes and examples which express rhetorical persuasion are not arguments proper to rhetoric only but are secondary demonstrations, syllogisms and inductions, which are also suitable for the purpose of rhetoric, the art of persuasion. Not all proofs referred to as ἀπόδειξις are philosophical proofs. For the purpose of speculative philosophy, then, demonstrative and dialectical proofs are those upon which Aristotle relies to attain knowledge of reality. The language of these proofs must be adequate to express this knowledge.

---

[20] *Poetics*, ch. 19; 1456a38-b1.
[21] *Ibid.*, ch. 6: 1450b11-12.
[22] "All that concerns Thought may be left to the treatise on Rhetoric, for the subject is more proper to that inquiry." ch. 19: 1456a33-36.
[23] *Physics* I: ch. 1; 184a9-16; *Met.* I: ch. 2; 982a5-7.

3.2.2 *Clarity and the Language of Proofs*

Although Aristotle uses ἀπόδειξις in the broad sense, apodeictic language or the language of proof, refers to the language of any of the arguments used by the philosopher, whether demonstrative or dialectical ones. This, however, still does not explain what are the restrictions regarding the language used in these arguments. It is obvious that the philosopher cannot phrase his opinions in a careless fashion. To be oblivious of the nuances of words is very often the reason why genuine reasoning is not effected:

For, since it is impossible to argue by introducing the actual things under discussion, but we use names as symbols in the place of the things, we think that what happens in the case of the names happens also in the case of the things, just as people who are counting think in the case of their counters. But the cases are not really similar; for names and a quantity of terms are finite, whereas things are infinite in number; and so the same expression and the single name must necessarily signify a number of things. As, therefore, in the above illustration, those who are not clever at managing the counters are deceived by the experts, in the same way in arguments also those who are unacquainted with the power of names are the victims of false reasoning, both when they are themselves arguing and when they are listening to others.[24]

Indeed, it is the meanings and definitions of words to which Aristotle first turns his attention in philosophy, but it is important to note that Aristotle in this passage intends his words to refer to things. Unless a word has a meaning, it cannot be used meaningfully in a proposition. Yet this is not to say that men must learn definitions or precise meanings before using words. This would not respect the process by which, as Aristotle affirms and all men experience, men come to knowledge. This process Aristotle applies both to our ideas and to our language; the process of going from the confused to the distinct:

... What is to us plain and obvious is at first rather confused masses ... Much the same thing happens in the relation of the name to the formula. A name, e.g. 'round', means vaguely a sort of whole: its definition analyzes this into its particular senses. Similarly a child begins by calling all men 'father', and all women 'mother', but later on distinguishes each of them.[25]

---

[24] *Soph. Ref.* I: ch. 1; 164a22-23; 165a1-18.
[25] *Physics* I: ch. 1; 184a21 ff.

One may use a word before its precise meaning is distinguished; he may know one or some of the objects to which it refers or he may have witnessed the success of others who used such words. Initially, its meaning is confused; one may associate it with an insufficient number of things or with the wrong things. Yet there is some meaning, even if confused, in the mind of the one who speaks. This is not yet the stage at which one will be proficient in using words in argumentation.

To say that a word must have meaning in philosophy is possibly to say no more than that a word must be a word, or at least a name. Such is a requirement for any intelligent communication. What is important in philosophical usage of words is the *kind* of meaning that they must have. It is our purpose now to determine what Aristotle says about the language of proof. Although we have indicated that rhetorical and poetical proofs are not the instruments of speculative philosophy, we will begin by examining the language used in these proofs. Then, by contrast, it will be clearer what kind of language Aristotle admits in dialectical and demonstrative proofs.

3.2.2.1 *Rhetoric and Poetry*

In examining Aristotle's words beginning with the *Poetics* and the *Rhetoric*, it will be useful to keep in mind that we are attempting to determine the kinds of words and the kinds of meaning that Aristotle specifies for philosophical usage. This is first pointed out in the *Rhetoric* and *Poetics*. There Aristotle considers a point that he does not even advert to in the works of the *Organon* — the element of style. We have seen that the purpose of poetry and rhetoric is such and its audience is of such a character that, as Aristotle says "it is not sufficient to know what one ought to say, but one must also know how to say it, and this largely contributes to making the speech appear of a certain character".[26]

---

[26] *Rhet.* III: ch. 1; 1403b15-18. "...for it does make a difference, for the purpose of making a thing clear, to speak in this or that manner ..." *Rhet.* III: ch. 1; 1404a8-10; "...it is of great importance owing to the corruption of the hearer." *Rhet.* III: ch. 1; 1404a7-8.

As we have seen, Aristotle in chapters nineteen and twenty of the *Poetics* makes the purely grammatical distinctions preliminary to a consideration of representation in poetry and accessory to rhetorical arguments. After these grammatical distinctions, Aristotle treats the choice of words proper to poetry and to rhetoric. To what kinds of words and meanings does Aristotle limit linguistic usage in these arts?

In Chapter twenty-one of the *Poetics*, Aristotle divides nouns[27] according as they are either ordinary (κύριον), rare, metaphorical, ornamental, invented, lengthened, curtailed, or altered.[28] Twining interprets these not as species of nouns excluding each other (simple and compound are the species of nouns) but as distinct properties of words, several of which may subsist together in the same word: "The extended word may be metaphorical, foreign, or both. None of these may be at the same time common."[29]

Aristotle customarily designates words other than common (κύριον) as ξενικός or foreign, unfamiliar: "By 'unfamiliar' I mean a rare use."[30] Aristotle also opposes the foreign or unfamiliar words to customary (εἰωθός) words as when he notes that epithets may be used in poetry to a certain extent because they remove the style from the ordinary (εἰωθός) and give a "foreign" air (ξενικὴν),[31] and again, "What we have said will make the style pleasant, if it contains a happy mixture of proper (ειωθός) and 'foreign' (ξενικόν) words, of rhythm, and of persuasiveness resulting from propriety."[32]

These remarks of Aristotle occasion two questions. Are the common (κύριον) the same as the customary words (εἰωθός), for both are, at different times, opposed to foreign words? Is the proper (οἰκείον) the same as the common word and/or the cus-

---

[27] ὄνομα here refers to verbs, adverbs, and nouns or the directly significant parts of language. Cf. Bywater, *op. cit.*, p. 175 on *Poetics*, 1450b14.
[28] *Poetics* ch. 21: 1457a31.
[29] Thomas Twining, *Aristotle's Treatise on Poetry* (London: Payne and Son, 1789), p. 449, n. 21.
[30] *Poetics* ch. 21: 1458a22.
[31] *Rhet.* III: ch. 3; 1406a15.
[32] *Ibid.*, ch. 12: 1414a26.

tomary word? It is difficult to determine the answer because
Aristotle does not confine his usage to strict meanings of words.
In the *Poetics*, Aristotle notes that in iambic poetry Aeschylus and
Euripides wrote the same line with the change of one word only,
"a rare (γλῶτταν) in place of one made ordinary by custom (κύριον
εἰωθότος)."[33] Custom, evidently, adds something to common
words in the strict sense. Twining notes that the word ἐσθίει does
not mean strictly common but only a common metaphor, that is,
a word which though originally metaphorical had acquired by
constant use the effect of a proper word. He would distinguish
between the common words in the general sense and proper
(οἰκεῖον) words: "What we call proper words are only one sort
of the κύρια ὀνόματα of Aristotle. The expression must even include all those words, which though originally metaphorical, are ...
'so naturalized' by common use, 'that ceasing to be metaphors, they
are become, (as it were), the proper words," for example, 'foot of
the mountain' and 'bed of the river'.[34] It is possible at this point
to conclude that words that are made ordinary by custom add
naturalized metaphors (and even possibly other naturalized foreign
words) to the strictly common (κύριον) words which are the same
as proper (οἰκεῖον) words. We have, then, the common (κύριον)
words in the broad sense which include the proper (οἰκεῖον) words
and the words made ordinary by custom, (κύριον εἰωθότος). Both
of these, proper words and words made ordinary by custom, are
referred to as common words.

The fundamental point of style common to rhetoric and poetry
is clarity. In every case, Aristotle identifies clarity in style basically
with the use of the common words. But he does not limit either
ordinary conversation or the diction of poetry and rhetoric to
common words. In addition to clarity, poetic diction must not
be commonplace but rather elevated in proportion to the subject:
"The merit of diction is to be clear and not commonplace."[35] In
rhetoric the diction must be clear but neither commonplace nor

---

[33] *Poetics* ch. 22: 1458b18.
[34] Twining, *op. cit.*, p. 462, n. 204; p. 434, n. 179.
[35] *Poetics* ch. 22: 1458a18.

elevated:

In regard to style, one of its chief merits may be defined as perspicuity. This is
shown by the fact that the speech, if it does not make the meaning clear, will
not perform its proper function; neither must it be mean, nor above the dignity
of the subject, but appropriate to it; for the poetic style may be is not mean,
but it is not appropriate to prose.[36]

Both poetry and rhetoric admit of pleasurable accessories to language which do not impede clarity and are proportionate to the
subject:

Tragedy is, then, a representation of an action that is heroic and complete and
of a certain magnitude — by means of language enriched with all kinds of
ornament, each used separately in the different parts of the play;[37]

... as a matter of right, one should aim at nothing more in a speech than how
to avoid exciting pain and pleasure. For justice should consist in fighting the
case with the facts alone, so that everything else that is beside demonstration
is superfluous; nevertheless, as we have just said, it (style and delivery) is of
great importance owing to the corruption of the hearer... but all these things
are mere outward show for pleasing the hearer; wherefore no one teaches geometry in this way.[38]

We have noted that in both rhetoric and poetry clarity is identified basically with the use of common words. What kind of words,
beyond the common ones, may be admitted to prevent common-
placeness without impeding clarity? A common word is the usual,
established term for expressing anything, opposed to the foreign,
barbarous, archaic or obsolete term.[39] But if poetic diction consists only of common words, it will be commonplace. It is the
foreign or unfamiliar words — those beyond ordinary use — that
must be used to lend dignity; yet to write entirely in these uncom-
mon words will result in riddle or jargon: "We need then a sort
of mixture of the two. For the one kind will save the diction from
being prosaic and common place, the rare word, for example, and
the metaphor and the 'ornament', whereas the ordinary words will
give clarity."[40]

[36]   *Rhet.* III: ch. 2; 1404b1.
[37]   *Poetics* ch. 6: 1449b20.
[38]   *Rhet.* III: ch. 1; 1404a3; parenthesis mine.
[39]   Cope, *The Rhetoric of Aristotle with a Commentary*, III, p. 18 on *Rhet.* III:
ch. 2; 1404b26.
[40]   *Poetics* ch. 22: 1458a22.

Clarity and distinction are also enhanced in poetry by the lengthening, abbreviation and alteration of words, the clarity being preserved by retaining part of the usual form of the word. Of course the principle of moderation is invoked in all cases in order that the result will not be ridiculous.[41] A greater restriction is made for iambic poetry than for the other types since iambic is largely an imitation of ordinary conversation. Only those words, therefore, that are used in ordinary speech — the common word, the metaphor, and the ornament may be used in iambic.[42] Such is an improved imitation of common speech.[43]

The choice of words proper to rhetorical argument differs from that of poetry inasmuch as the subject is less elevated. No great departure from ordinary language should be made, "... of these (nouns and verbs) we should use strange, compound, or coined words only rarely and in a few places ... proper (κύριον) and appropriate (οἰκεῖον) words and metaphors are alone to be employed in the style of prose; this is shown by the fact that no one employs anything but these." These are the words, Aristotle claims, that everyone uses in conversation. Although it is the common word that produces clarity, the orator should use a sufficiency of metaphors to give a foreign air to the diction but not so much that it becomes ornate.[44] This demands greater attention to metaphors in prose since it has fewer means of expression than verse does. The word in this passage which is translated as proper is κύριον; the appropriate words are the οἰκεῖον or κύριον in the strict sense as opposed to metaphor.[45] The three — proper, appropriate, and metaphor — do not, then, seem to be mutually exclusive.

To summarize, we have seen that the elevated subject matter of poetry admits the use of common, rare, metaphorical and ornamental words. Iambic poetry, an improved imitation of ordinary conversation, allows only the common, metaphorical and orna-

---

[41] *Ibid.*, 1458b1.
[42] *Poetics* ch. 22: 1459a13; *Rhet.* III: ch. 1; 1404a33.
[43] Twining, *op. cit.*, p. 467, n. 209.
[44] *Rhet.* III: ch. 2; 1404b5.
[45] Bywater, *op. cit.*, p. 279; Cope, *The Rhetoric of Aristotle with a Commentary*, III, p. 18; Twining, *op. cit.*, p. 433, n. 179.

mental. Rhetoric, which approaches ordinary conversation, uses the common, the appropriate and metaphorical words.

What we now see is that although Aristotle speaks of ordinary words as basic in poetry and rhetoric, their tediousness is alleviated by the more ornamental words proper to each art. In both arts the use of metaphor, as opposed to common words, is appropriate; its use in prose is not exactly as liberal as it is in poetry, however. Metaphor, the device for perfect poetic diction, must be adapted to the prose style of one finding arguments for persuasion. It must be neither too ornamental nor too far-fetched, but proportionate to the subject. Given these characteristics, it provides prose with the clarity necessary for persuasion through the three kinds of rhetorical arguments.

We have not yet explained, however, precisely what metaphor is. Aristotle often refers to a usage as metaphorical but only in the *Poetics* does he give a definition of metaphor. "Metaphor is the application of a strange term either transferred from the genus and applied to the species[46] or from the species and applied to the genus,[47] or from one species to another[48] or else by analogy."[49] What is otherwise a common term becomes, when used to name something to which its definition or meaning does not refer, a metaphor. The correct and artistic use of metaphor indicates an eye for resemblances in the one who uses it. It is the pleasure provided by the perception and representation of similarity in what is dissimilar that justifies the use of metaphor in poetry and rhetoric.

It is of interest to note that in *Poetry* and *Rhetoric* equivocation

[46] For example, " 'Here *stands* my ship.' Riding at anchor is a species of standing."
[47] "Indeed *ten thousand* noble things Odysseus did, for ten thousand, which is a species of many, is here used instead of the word 'many'."
[48] " '*Drawing off* his life with the bronze' and '*Severing* with the tireless bronze', where 'drawing off' is used for 'severing' and 'severing' for 'drawing off', both being species of 'removing'."
[49] "... when B is to A as D is to C, then instead of B the poet will say D and B instead of D." *Poetics* ch. 21: 1457b9.

is never mentioned. Yet if what Aristotle says in *Prior Analytics* about the enthymeme and the example holds when these arguments are used in rhetoric and poetry, then does not the prohibition of equivocation in such arguments apply to them in rhetoric and poetry? There is reason for answering this in the negative. As we have seen, the character of rhetoric and poetry and of their audience is such that style is important, and this even in the expression of the logical arguments. We assume this to mean that even the logical enthymemes and examples may be couched in the style appropriate to each art — which includes for rhetoric the use of common, metaphorical and ornamental words and for poetry, the use of the ordinary, metaphorical and rare words.

3.2.2.2 *Demonstration and Dialectic*

Aristotle aims at clarity or lack of obscurity in philosophy. What he means by clarity he does not state formally in any one place. From his remarks we may conclude that clarity will be achieved in philosophy by avoiding equivocation, ambiguity, and metaphor.

In discussing the language used in dialectical and demonstrative proofs of philosophy, Aristotle does not do his reader the favor, as he has in the *Poetics* and *Rhetoric*, of indicating whether such language should consist of common ordinary words and what the criterion of ordinary words is. What he has to say about language is discussed in terms of clarity of meaning and the avoidance both of equivocation and of the use of metaphor. Aristotle has defined equivocation or equivocal words in the *Categories* as words that have the name in common, the definition corresponding with the name being different. The example he gives is that of man and the portrait of a man; both can properly be called "animals" equivocally, for they have the name only in common, the definitions being different. There are three modes connected with equivocation and ambiguity:

(1) when the expression or name properly signifies more than one thing, such as ἀετός and κύων, (2) when we customarily (εἰωθότες) use a word in more

than one sense, (3) when a word has more than one meaning in combination
with another word, though by itself it has only one meaning, for example,
'knowing letters'; for it may so happen that taken separately 'knowing' and
'letters' have only one meaning, namely, either that the letters themselves have
knowledge or that someone else has knowledge of the letters.[50]

Precision of language is what Aristotle requires for successful communication in philosophy. No equivocation or ambiguity of meaning is allowed. Two discussants may not be directing their minds
to the same thing unless the different senses of the word have been
made clear beforehand. It is important to note here that the philosopher clarifies language so that his discussion will bear on one
thing.

For if the various ways in which a term can be used are not clear, it is possible
that the answerer and the questioner are not applying their mind to the same
thing; ... For if we know the various senses in which a term can be used, we
shall never be misled by false reasoning, but we shall be aware of it if the questioner fails to direct his argument to the same point, ...[51]

It is possible also for a single definition to be equivocal; definitions,
therefore, should be examined for ambiguity. For example, if one
states that what denotes and what produces health are "commensurably related to health", we must examine what he has meant
by "commensurably" in each case; whether in the latter case it
means "of the requisite quality to produce health", whereas in the
former case it means "of the requisite quality to denote of what
kind the state is which is present".[52] It is clear from this example
what Aristotle means by clarity of meaning.

3.2.3   *Confusion of Meaning: The Sophists; Plato*

Aristotle charges both the Sophists and Plato, among others, with
violating this clarity by failing to clarify their meanings. On the
basis of this he refuses to admit the Sophists as philosophers;
Plato, however, is one of his philosophical predecessors. It is easy

---

[50]   *Soph. Ref.* ch. 4: 166a16-22.
[51]   *Topics* I: ch. 18; 108a27-31.
[52]   *Topics* I: ch. 15; 107a6.

to see the difference here. The Sophists are interested not in attaining any truth about reality but only in achieving the appearance of wisdom and this by means of linguistic sleight.[53] This moral purpose immediately excludes them from the circle of philosophers. Their linguistic tricks consist in using their terms either with more than one meaning or with a confused meaning. Because they are not interested in the referents of their words or the assertion of truth or falsity about these referents, ambiguity of meaning not only need not be avoided by them, is it their weapon.

Aristotle's most formal statement about definite meaning is to be found in connection with the defense of the principle of contradiction against the sophistic attacks. Because words directly signify things understood, unless a word has a definite meaning, it will signify confused thought and will not refer to any definite thing. Confused signification is of no value in philosophy:

... the proper beginning for all such debates is not a demand for some undeniable assertion that something is or is not... but a demand for expressing the same idea to oneself and to another; for this much is necessary, if there is to be any proposition at all. If a person does not do even this, he is not talking either to himself or to another... not to have some specific meaning is to have no meaning, then when words have no meaning, conversation with another, and indeed with oneself has been annihilated, since it is impossible for one who does not think something to think anything. Let us suppose, therefore, what we supposed in the beginning, that a word has a meaning and a specific meaning.[54]

In the case of the most basic principle of knowledge the words "be" and "not be" must signify something determinate; not everything can be so and also not so.[55]

Plato, on the other hand, has set himself the task of finding the elements of all things, a task which is impossible for one reason because he has not distinguished the senses in which all things are said to be.[56] It is impossible to find the elements or principles of

[53] *Soph. Ref.* ch. 1: 165a20-25; ch. 11: 171b26-35; *Met.* IV: ch. 2; 1004b18-26.
[54] *Met.* IV: ch. 4; 1006a18; b8.
[55] *Met.* IV: ch. 4; 1006a29 ff.
[56] The other reason why Plato's task is impossible is because an all-embracing science like Plato's dialectic which proves the whole nature of reality is impossible because a science cannot be demonstrative throughout but must start with immediately known premisses; it is also evident that such a science cannot

things unless the multiplicity of meanings is divided and made
definite.[57] Things whose definitions differ will have different principles. The Ideas, then, cannot be the principles of all things because all things do not exist in the same way; therefore, they cannot
have the same kind of principles.

In contrast to Plato, Aristotle divides and makes precise the
meanings of "being" according as things exist:

> ... 'being', too, has various meanings, but they all refer back to a single root:
> somethings are said to 'be' because they are themselves primary beings; others,
> because they modify primary beings; still others, because they are on the way
> to becoming a being, or are destroying it, or are its defects or its qualities or
> its producers or sources or what ever may be relative to a primary being or to
> the negation of such a being or of its relations. Thus, we declare even nonbeing
> to 'be' what-is-not.[58]

It is easy to see from the cases of the Sophists and Plato why Aristotle demands definite meanings in philosophy. If a word can be
said in many ways, its referent will not always be the same. Unless
the philosopher specifies which sense of the word he intends, there
can be only an obscure idea about that to which he refers, "... not
to have some specific meaning is to have no meaning". In such a
case communication is impossible.

3.2.4   Metaphors: Plato; Empedocles

Besides the prohibition of ambiguity, Aristotle specifically forbids
the use of metaphor in establishing the definitions which are the
principles of demonstration. In comparing and selecting common

---

have been present in us from birth, else why are we unaware of it. Cf. *Met.* I:
ch. 9. The same criticism applies to Parmenides; cf. *Physics* I: ch. 3; 186a23-34;
Met. I: ch. 5; 986b19-987a2.

[57]   "In general, if we search for the elements of things without distinguishing
the various senses in which the latter are said to be, it will be impossible to find
them; especially if we search in this manner for the elements of which things
are composed. For it is surely impossible to grasp of what doing is composed,
or undergoing, or the straight; but this is feasible, if at all, only in the case of
primary beings. Therefore it is not true to say that we may seek, or rightly
think that we have, the elements of all things." *Met.* I: ch. 9; 992b18-24.

[58]   *Met.* IV: ch. 2; 1003b4-11.

elements, "clearly metaphors and metaphorical expressions are precluded in definition: otherwise dialectic would involve metaphors".[59] Neither should a metaphorical expression be given as a genus of definition for a genus is always predicated of its species in its literal sense (κύριον). For example, "harmony" should not be given as the genus of temperance, for it is predicated of temperance not in a literal sense but metaphorically, for a harmony always consists in notes.[60] Because the task of definition is to make something known, the language used in definition should be as clear as possible. This means that the meaning or definition of a term should refer properly to that to which the name is applied. For example, the meaning of "harmony" refers to a relation among musical notes; "harmony", therefore, if used as a genus of temperance will not provide the clarity necessary to explain what temperance is.

The question arises whether use of metaphor in reasoning cannot be considered a mode of equivocation. Equivocation occurs in discussion when a name has more than one meaning thereby referring possibly to more than one thing. A word used metaphorically refers to that which its meaning signifies as well as to that to which it is secondarily transferred in a given instance. For example, the word "harmony" will refer to a relationship among notes and, used metaphorically, to describe the virtue of temperance. Everything that can be said about the causes and properties of notes as harmonious, however, cannot be said of temperance as a harmony. The same is true of "evening" used to refer to a time of day and metaphorically to old age. All that can be said of evening as time of day surely cannot be said of old age. The fallacy of equivocation occurs because different meanings refer to different things. In such a case argument or discussion does not bear on one definite thing. It seems, then, that the use of metaphor is a mode of equivocation, and for that reason, is excluded from philosophical arguments.

It is the use of metaphors by Plato in expressing his theory of

[59]   *Post. An.* II: ch. 13; 97b37-39.
[60]   *Top.* IV: ch. 3; 123a33.

ideas that demands Aristotle's rejection of the theory. Plato draws an analogy between the production of natural things and the production of artificial things, patterning the former on the latter. In this way he sees sensible things as "coming from" the Ideas. This, for Aristotle, is a purely metaphorical use of the expression "to come from".[61] Men speak of "coming from" in its ordinary senses as either (1) coming from a material, (2) coming from a starting point of movement, (3) from the matter and form of another individual, (4) coming of the form from its parts, as a syllable from letters, (5) coming of one thing from part of another — as in the case of human generation, or (6) coming of one thing from another in time — as night from day.[62] In none of these senses can sensible things be said to "come from" the Ideas; the analogy simply does not hold and the metaphor is incorrect. An artist referring to an exemplar still depends on material and his own agency for production of his artistic result. Plato has failed to give a meaning to "coming from" so that his theory may be understood.

Let us return for a moment to Empedocles' use of the terms "love and strife" to refer to the principles of unity and disunity both in the cosmos and among men. Is such a use metaphorical? Aristotle does not explicitly refer to it as metaphor. Whether or not it is metaphorical language depends on whether Empedocles was drawing an analogy between the cosmos and man or whether the distinction between the two had yet been made. If Empedocles had not recognized the distinction between man and the cosmos, then the meaning of love and strife is obscure, its definition referring to human emotions being applied also to the cosmos — a confused term in that its definition applies to more than one thing. If, on the other hand, Empedocles does see the distinction between the cosmos and man but is drawing an analogy between them, his analogy is incorrect and the application of the terms "love and

---

[61] "In addition, other things do not come 'from' the ideas in any of the usual senses of 'from'. But to say that the ideas are patterns and that other things participate in them is to use empty words and poetical metaphors." *Met.* I: ch. 9; 991a20.

[62] *Met.* V: ch. 24; 1023a25-b8.

strife" to the cosmos is a metaphor or extension of the term. If it is this, then it does not properly refer to the unity and disunity in the cosmos. What Empedocles needs is to redefine his terms.

We have noted now that predication in the language of demonstration is limited to the literal as opposed to metaphorical. The predication of common meanings is what is desired in what we may call the literal language of philosophy. Although a judicious use of metaphor is allowed in poetical and rhetorical composition, the use of metaphor is excluded from philosophical discourse. Now if ordinary conversation includes the use of metaphor, then philosophical language will not be as broad in scope as the language of ordinary conversation. If the purpose of philosophy is not simply to speak clearly but to achieve knowledge of reality, its principles and causes — and this is what it is for Aristotle — then this restriction of its language seems not only justified but desirable.

Aristotle allows confused meanings in the beginning of philosophy only.[63] Such is not Sophistic confusion of meaning, for Aristotle found his non-Sophistic predecessors engaged in the same task as he was: the attempt to gain knowledge of reality and its causes. Their confusion of language arose either from their incorrect analogies or from their failure to make distinctions.

3.2.5 *Words Said in Many Ways*

We have seen that clarity in philosophical arguments means the avoidance of equivocation and ambiguity including metaphor. Does this mean, however, that only univocal words may be used in philosophy?

3.2.5.1 *Pròs Hén Equivocals*

If Aristotle's division of words is equivocal and univocal, then we would reply affirmatively to this question, but when distinguishing the various meanings of one word, Aristotle sometimes denies that the words that are not univocal are purely equivocal:

[63] *Met.* I: ch. 10; 993a15.

Practically speaking, just as every other term which is used in several senses is so used owing to verbal coincidence or *because the different senses are derived from different prior meanings*, as it is also with 'contact'.[64]

What does Aristotle mean by words-said-in-many-ways which are not merely coincidental but are derived from different prior meanings?[65] If we examine what he says, we see that he places these non-coincidental words said in many ways midway between the equivocals and the univocal words of the *Categories*:

It follows, therefore, that there are three sorts of friendship, and that they are not all so termed in respect of one thing (καθ' ἕν) or as species of one genus, nor yet have they the same name entirely by accident (λέγεσθαι ομωνύμως). For all these uses of the term are related to one particular sort of friendship which is primary — as with the term 'surgical', — we speak of a surgical mind and a surgical instrument and a surgical operation, but we apply the term properly to that which is primarily so called.[66]

In the conclusion of this passage, Aristotle refers to the non-coincidental words said in many ways as "related to one thing": (πρὸς ἕν),

The only remaining alternative, therefore, is that in a sense the primary sort of friendship alone is friendship, but in a sense all sorts are, not as having a common name by accident and standing in a merely chance relationship to one another, not yet as falling under one species (καθ' ἕν), but rather as related to one thing. (πρὸς ἕν)[67]

Aristotle goes on to give a criterion for words said in many ways which are not entirely coincidental.

The primary is that of which the definition is implicit in the definition of all, for example, a surgical instrument is an instrument that a surgeon would use, whereas the definition of the instrument is not implicit in that of surgeon.[68]

Logical priority or priority in definition, then, is what is required for non-coincidental words said in many ways. There is some relation between the things named. Aristotle does not give a list

---

[64]   *De Gen.* I: ch. 6; 322b30-33.
[65]   *Topics* II: ch. 3; 110b16-19; Cf. also *Met.* XI: ch. 3; 1060b36-1061a7; IV: ch. 2; 1003a34-b5.
[66]   *Eud. Eth.* VII: ch. 2; 1236a16-18.
[67]   *Eud. Eth.* VII: ch. 2; 1236b24-27.
[68]   *Eud. Eth.* VII: ch. 2; 1236a20-24. Cf. also *Met.* XIII: ch. 2; 1077b3-4.

specifying precisely what the relations between these things named by the same name must be. Different relations occur in different instances. In the case of "healthy" the relation to health may be that of preserving or producing or being a sign of health.[69] In the case of things called "medical" they can either possess or be instruments for the art of medicine.[70] As for "being", things are called "being" because they modify substances, are on the way to becoming or destroying substances, or are its defects, qualities, producers or sources.[71] In other words, no specific relation or set of specific relations between two things is necessary for one to be named by reference to the other.[72] In virtue of whatever relation there is, the definition of what is logically prior is included in the definition of the thing to which the name is secondarily imposed.

Aristotle, as might be expected, does not mention logical priority as the criterion of *pròs hén* words every time he refers to it. Particularly in the *Topics*, reference to the criterion is lacking.[73] Owen argues from this that Aristotle, at the time of writing his early works, had not yet recognized the significance of focal meaning and had not yet formulated its formal characteristic of logical priority of the primary meaning of the word.[74]

We do not agree with Owen's argument here. In giving the reason let us note first that the examples of the fallacy of equivocation are often instances, according to Aristotle's division, of *pròs hén* as opposed to nonchance equivocation:

Those who know, learn; for it is those who know the use of letters that learn what is dictated to them.[75]

where "learn" means "understand by using knowledge" in one in-

---

[69] *Met.* IV: ch. 2; 1003a4-6; cf. also VII: ch. 1; IX: ch. 1; 1045b27-32.

[70] *Ibid.*, 1003b1-3.

[71] *Ibid.*, 1003a4-10.

[72] Cf. also *Eud. Eth.* VII: ch. 2; 1236a7-33.

[73] G. E. L. Owen, "Logic and Metaphysics in Some Earlier Works of Aristotle", *Aristotle and Plato in the Mid-Fourth Century*, ed. I. During and G. E. L. Owen (Goteburg: Almquist and Wiksell, 1960), pp. 173, n. 6; *Topics* I: ch. 15; 106b33-37; 107a5-12; ch. 9; 103b20-39.

[74] This interpretation, of course, is based on Owen's acceptance of the general theory of Aristotle's development. Cf. pp. 161-162.

[75] *Soph. Ref.* ch. 4: 165b3; cf. also *Topics* I: ch. 15; 107a5-7; 107b6-12.

stance and "acquire knowledge" in the other.[76] Does this necessarily mean that at the time of writing the *Topics* and *Sophistical
Refutations* Aristotle had not yet recognized or at least not realized
the significance of the distinction of nonchance equivocation and
words related by reference of one to the other? It does not seem
that this is the case if we examine the purpose of these two works.
In both works, Aristotle is concerned with avoiding ambiguity or
confusion of definitions. Words that are used in several senses
whether by chance or by reference (πρὸς ἕν) are capable of such
ambiguity if their definitions are not precisely given. Notice what
Aristotle has to say about the possible ambiguity of "health":

> Often too in the actual definitions the equivocal slips in unnoticed; therefore
> examination must be made of the definitions also. For example, if someone
> states that what denotes and what produces health are 'commensurably related
> to health', we must not shrink from the task but examine what he has meant
> by 'commensurably' in each case, for example, whether in the latter case it
> means that it is 'of the requisite quantity to produce health', whereas in the
> former case it means that it is 'of the requisite quality to denote of what kind
> the state is which is present.[77]

What is important is that fallacy be avoided by recognizing that
in the case of both nonchance equivocal words and *pròs hén* words,
there cannot be given one definition suitable for all uses of the
words. The fallacy of equivocation occurs in arguments when there
is an exchange, within one argument, of words whose definitions
are not wholly the same, whether or not they are partially the
same.[78] Different meanings will refer to different things. In such
a case the argument will not bear on the same thing. While this
is of no import for the Sophist, for the philosopher it is a basic
consideration.[79]

---

[76] Cf. also *Soph. Ref.* ch. 33: 182b22-28 on the ambiguity of "being" and
"unity".
[77] *Top.* I: ch. 15; 100b6-13.
[78] *Soph. Ref.* ch. 4: 165b30-166a7; *Cat.* ch. 1: 1a1 ff.
[79] One glaring omission of any reference to *pròs hén* as such occurs in *Topics*
IV: ch. 2; 139b2 where Aristotle gives examples of ambiguous words as (1)
equivocal, (2) words used in several senses, (3) metaphor as opposed to common
usage, (4) worse than metaphor which is not equivocal, metaphor, nor common,
and (5) unusual words. Since *pròs hén* is not mentioned here it may be argued,
as Owen does, that Aristotle was unaware of it at this time. But Aristotle is

For example, if the definitions are related *pròs hén* as substance
and accident called "beings" are, then the "being" said of each
cannot be interchanged or confused in one argument because
"being" is not predicated in the same way of everything.[80] So
"definition" will have a different meaning for primary being and
for one of the other predicates:

> For, though all things 'are', they 'are' not in the same way; but some things
> are primarily, and the rest dependently. So, also, the statement of what a thing
> is refers essentially to primary being; and to the other categories, only in some
> sense. We might ask even of a quality, What is it? so that even a quality is an
> instance of 'what' is, but not essentially.[81]

For this reason also it is useless, as Aristotle maintains against his
predecessors, to "search for the elements of things without distinguishing the various senses in which the latter are said to be, ..."[82]
In like manner one definition cannot be given of "healthy" for all
things are not healthy in the same way but some as the sign of
health and some as producing health. Yet in a given science what
is said of the word in its primary sense — whether "healthy" or
"being" — will apply in some modified sense to its other meanings.

We see here the necessity of precision of meaning before making
statements about things. Accidents "are" not in the same way that
substance "is". Before making a statement about being, one must
indicate whether he is talking about the being of substance or of
accidents.

Our point here has been to show that in the *Sophistical Refutations* and the *Topics*, Aristotle is concerned with the avoidance of
the fallacy of equivocation whether it results from nonchance equivocation or from the use of words related *pròs hén*. Contrary to

---

here considering what he has considered in various other contexts of the *Topics*;
the categories of words given here are not mutually exclusive since these categories differ from those given in other places in this same work. We use the
same argument here; a formal distinction of *pròs hén* is not necessary here, for
"several senses" is broad enough to cover *pròs hén*. As we shall see later, the
term "metaphor" is broad enough to cover it also.
[80] *Met.* III: ch. 3; 998b22 ff.
[81] *Met.* VII: ch. 4; 1030a18-26.
[82] *Met.* I: ch. 9; 992b18-20.

Owen's claim, it does not seem necessary for him in this context to specify the exact criterion of *pròs hén légomena* words.

We may now draw some conclusions regarding Aristotle's use of terminology in the context of equivocation. What Aristotle refers to as equivocation or words said in many ways (πολλαχῶς λέγομενα) includes two kinds: (1) equivocation by chance, and (2) words related *pròs hén*. Both of these kinds may be and are, at times, referred to be the generic names of either equivocation or πολλαχῶς λεγόμενα.

3.2.5.2   *The Meaning of Metaphor*

We have indicated now the difference between pure equivocation and *pròs hén* usage of words and that in both cases either the failure to specify precise meanings or the interchange of meanings in one argument constitutes the fallacy of equivocation — the chief impediment to the clarity necessary in arguments.

Yet we can still note what appears, at least, to be an inconsistency in Aristotle's usage. While rejecting, as we have seen, the poetical metaphors and lisping expressions of his predecessors, as improper language for arguments, Aristotle himself refers to some of his own usages as metaphorical. In the *Metaphysics*, the use of "nature" to name any substance whatever, is referred to as metaphorical. If we recall the definition of metaphor in the *Poetics*: "Metaphor is the application of a strange term ..."[83] and the prohibition of the use of metaphor in philosophical arguments because it prevents clarity and constitutes equivocation, then we must question how Aristotle can permit a metaphorical use of "nature" in the statements of metaphysics. What, we may ask, is the meaning of "metaphorical" in this passage?

Book Five of the *Metaphysics* is devoted to clarifying the meanings of *pròs hén* terms which will be used in metaphysics. In examining the term "nature" Aristotle gives five meanings and two additional meanings. Nature means (1) the generation of growing things, (2) the intrinsic principle of birth and growth out of which

---

[83]   ch. 21: 1457b9.

a thing begins to grow; (3) the intrinsic principle of motion and rest; (4) the matter out of which a thing is made; first matter in general or particular; (5) the form or substance of natural things. To this last meaning he adds a metaphorical use of the word: "By an extension of meaning (μεταφορᾷ) from this last sense of 'nature' every substance in general has come to be called a 'nature', because the nature of a thing is one kind of a substance.[84] St. Thomas points out that as the term of generation is called nature, so since the term of generation is a substance, every kind of substance may be called a nature. "Nature", therefore, is among the names of the common things considered in metaphysics.[85] Although referring to this as a metaphorical use of the term, Aristotle includes this use of "nature" in those meanings that can be referred to the first and proper meaning of "nature": "... the essence of things which have in themselves, as such, a source of movement."[86]

If Aristotle includes the metaphorical meaning of "nature" among those that are referred to the first meaning, then clearly this is a *pròs hén* signification and use of the word. How can *pròs hén* be identified with metaphor as the foregoing text demands? The passage seems to indicate that the term μεταφορὰ must be, at times, broad enough to include *pròs hén*. Such a meaning of μεταφορὰ then will signify simply the extension of a name in general whether that name is a metaphor in the sense of the *Poetics* or a *pròs hén* equivocal defined with reference to the definition of another word.[87]

To obtain further knowledge of what Aristotle may intend by "metaphor" and its relation to *pròs hén* equivocals, let us look at the passage on the meaning of "potency". Aristotle gives four meanings of "power" or "potency": (1) the external source of a movement or change in a thing; or, if internal, a distinct otherness in the thing moved (active potency); (2) the principle whereby something is moved or changed by another as other (passive potency);

---

[84] *Met.* V: ch. 4; 1015a11-12.
[85] *In Met.* V: less. 5; #823.
[86] *Met.* V: ch. 4; 1015a13-14.
[87] For this explanation of metaphor, see Ralph M. McInerny, "Metaphor and Analogy", *Sciences Ecclésiastiques*, XVI (Mai-Septembre, 1964), 287.

(3) the principle of performing an act well or according to intention; (4) the tendency to remain impassive, or to resist change for the worse. The last three meanings of "potency" refer to the first:

Possibilities in the sense of potencies all relate to the first meaning given, that is, to a source of things that is external or distinct. Other things are called 'capable', some because something else has such power over them; some because nothing has such power over them; and some because there is a power over them in some way or other.[88]

Aristotle gives four corresponding meanings of "ability" or "capacity" and "incapacity" as well as the sense of "impossible" and "possible".[89] At the end he adds a metaphorical sense of "power": "The term 'power' is also used metaphorically (κατὰ μεταφορὰν) in geometry." But this meaning of "power", although one of several ways in which the word can be said (λέγεται πολλαχῶς), is dismissed from metaphysics as an equivocal mode, for it is called "power" only by a likeness.[90]

What is this likeness according to which the square of a line is called a power? St. Thomas explains that "...just as from something in potency something actual comes to be, in a similar way from multiplying a line by itself its square results.[91] ... the root of a square bears some likeness to the matter from which a thing is made; and for this reason the root is said to be capable of becoming its square as matter is capable of becoming a thing."[92]

It is clear that this is not simply a metaphorical use of "power" in the *Poetics'* sense of metaphor where a name which belongs to something else is used to name another thing. "Power" as it is used in geometry has its own commonly recognized definition; it cannot be said to be a name that belongs to something else. But neither is it a *pròs hén* equivocal although Aristotle refers to it as equivocal, and because it is not, Aristotle excludes it from the senses used in metaphysics:

---

[88] *Met.* V: ch. 12; 1019b34-20a4.
[89] *Ibid.*, 1019a15-b32.
[90] *Ibid.*, IX: ch. 1; 1046a4-7.
[91] *In V Met.*, less. 14; #974.
[92] *Ibid.*, less. 1, #1774.

Now, we have pointed out that there are several ways (λέγεται πολλαχῶς) in which we can speak of power and capability. Of these, we may dismiss those powers that are so called by an equivocation; for some are so called by analogy (likeness), as in geometry ...[93]

It is not a *pròs hén* equivocal because it is not, as the other *pròs hén* senses of "power" are, referred to the primary meaning of "power", the active principle of change in some other thing inasmuch as it is other.

3.2.5.3 *The Division of Words*

Boethius has given us a division of the words used by Aristotle as (1) pure equivocal or equivocal *a casu* or by chance; (2) equivocal *a consilio* or by design; and (3) univocal. Equivocal *a consilio* are those *pròs hén* names which, by the agreement of men, have definitions that are not exactly the same, but not entirely different. The modes of equivocals *a consilio*, according to Boethius are as follows:

(1) equivocal according to a similitude; as the picture of a man and a true man are called animals;
(2) equivocal according to a proportion; as principle means unity in number as well as point in a line;
(3) equivocal *ab uno*; as a medical instrument and a medical complexion are so called from their relation to medicine;
(4) equivocal *ad unum*; as riding is called healthy and food is called healthy, both as the cause of health.[94]

We see immediately that equivocals (3) *ab uno* and (4) *ad unum* correspond to the *pròs hén* equivocals spoken of earlier in which the definition of the primary meaning of the word is referred to in the definition of the secondary meanings. What, however, of the equivocals according to a similitude and according to a proportion? It seems that either of these may be the equivocal according to a *likeness* which "power" in geometry is. While it is not to our purpose here to examine every instance of such equivocals to determine whether they fulfill the criterion of *pròs hén* equivocation, it is easy to see in the examples Boethius gives that they do so. The definition of man surely is referred to in the definition of a picture

[93] *Met.* IX: ch. 1; 1046a4-7; parenthesis mine.
[94] Boethius, *In Categorias Aristotelis*, ed. Migne, *Patrologia Latina*, vol. 64, col. 166B-C.

of a man. Whatever meaning of principle is prior is referred to in the meaning of the secondary sense. Our problem is where, in this division, does an equivocal such as the use of "power" in geometry fit? Surely, on the basis of its being named by a likeness to "power" in the first sense, it cannot be equivocal *a casu*. If equivocal *a consilio* is coextensive with *pròs hén*, then "power" as used in geometry cannot fit there, for its definition does not refer to the first sense of "power". It seems, tentatively, that Boethius' equivocal *a consilio* can be broadened to include not only *pròs hén* equivocals but also metaphorical words whose definitions have no reference to the definition of the word from which they were originally extended. In noticing the likeness between the relation of a line and its square and a potency and its actuality, the capacity of a line to be squared can be called its power without any reference to the definition of an active potency.

3.3 CONCLUSION

The language of proof means explanation by real, not fictional causes. In addition, the demonstrative and dialectical proofs of philosophy exclude (1) ambiguous words and (2) equivocal words including metaphors whose definitions do not refer to that which they are metaphorically imposed to name. Because his non-Sophistic predecessors used such metaphors and ambiguous terms, Aristotle rejected their solutions although he accepted the integrity of the task in which they were engaged. But words said in many ways are not completely excluded from philosophy provided their exact meanings are clearly given. *Pròs hén* equivocals, in fact, draw attention to the relationship between the realities that they name. In one place, Aristotle tells us that whatever is said in reference to a single nature is a single science. It is this doctrine of *pròs hén* equivocals that enables Aristotle, as we shall see in the next chapter, to formulate the highest science.

A USE OF LANGUAGE: THE MEANING OF "BEING"

4.1 INTRODUCTION

It is our purpose in this chapter to examine an instance of Aristotle's use of language in philosophy and to indicate how he is concerned not solely with linguistic clarification but with positive knowledge of non-linguistic reality. We have seen in chapter two that Aristotle has a triadic theory of signification: words are symbols of concepts which are signs of things.[1] We have noted further that Aristotle, in philosophy, claims to be concerned with finding the principles and causes of real things.[2] Lastly, in chapter three we noted that Aristotle is dissatisfied both with the use of fictions as principles of explanation and with explanations by means of words whose meanings do not clearly refer to definite things.[3]

In making this last point in chapter three, we noticed that Aristotle formulated a *pròs hén* theory of meaning to explain the relationship of related meanings that are not univocal nor wholly equivocal.[4] It is by means of this *pròs hén* unity of meaning that Aristotle unifies the subject of the science of metaphysics.[5] It is to the theory of metaphysics unified according to a linguistic criterion that we wish to turn our attention now. Admittedly, in Aristotle's philosophy, it is merely one instance of dependence on the way men speak, but it is, we believe, an important one. Aris-

[1] pp. 34ff.
[2] pp. 40ff.
[3] Ch. 3, pp. 47-49.
[4] *Ibid.*, pp. 67ff.
[5] *Ibid.*, pp. 71, 76.

totle himself regarded metaphysics as the only science which was divine science.[6] His methodical elaboration of the *aporiae* at the beginning of the *Metaphysics* — a procedure that he did not employ so systematically in any other work — testifies to his concern for the possibility of this important science. If it is true as Charlesworth contends that Aristotle arrives at no positive knowledge of reality but merely dispels doubts and confusions,[7] then is Aristotle realizing his own project of a science of principles and causes of all reality? Or if it is correct, as has been maintained,[8] that "being *qua* being" has no foundation in reality other than the discourse we hold upon it, then Aristotle's endeavor is merely one of clarifying language.

That it is Aristotle's purpose in this science to speak about reality and not merely to clarify our speech about reality is patent in his own explanation of his project:

Clearly, then, wisdom is rational knowledge concerning certain basic factors and principles. Since this is the knowledge we are seeking, we must inquire of what sort the reasons and principles are which to know is wisdom."[9]

For we claim to know a thing only when we believe that we have discovered what primarily accounts for its being.[10]

In the *aporiae*, also, Aristotle wonders about the principles of primary beings, that is, whether all primary beings pertain to the

---

[6] "This science alone may be divine, and in a double sense: for a science which God would most appropriately have is divine among the sciences; and one whose object is divine, if such there be, is likewise divine. Now our science has precisely these two aspects: on the one hand, God is thought to be one of the reasons for all things and to be in some sense a beginning; on the other hand, this kind of science would be the only kind or the most appropriate kind for God to have. All other sciences, then, are more necessary than this; but none is more excellent." *Met.* I: ch. 2; 983a4-11.

[7] Maxwell John Charlesworth, *Philosophy and Linguistic Analysis* (Pittsburg: Duquesne University, 1959), pp. 208-215. Charlesworth rejects the view that the object of philosophy is clarification but accepts therapeutic clarification as the method of philosophy. This process, however, according to Charlesworth, proceeds mainly in a negative fashion without proving or explaining.

[8] Pierre Aubenque, *op. cit.*, "... because being *qua* being is not met, is not the object of any intuition neither sensible nor intellectual, it has no other foundation in reality than the discourse we hold upon it." p. 236. Aubenque, therefore, holds that metaphysics is not a science of being *qua* being.

[9] *Met.* I: ch. 1; 982a2-ch. 2; 982a5.

[10] *Ibid.*, ch. 3; 983a23-25. Cf. also Physics I: ch. 1; 184a10-15.

consideration of the metaphysician[11] and whether both sensible and nonsensible beings have the same principles.[12] Such matters as these are hardly formulated by one whose interest is only language clarification.

It is our purpose in this chapter to indicate how Aristotle is speaking of non-linguistic reality when he refers to the subject of metaphysics as being *qua* being, and how he gives positive knowledge of that subject. Let us turn now to the texts of central importance for this.

Aristotle states the criterion for unity of metaphysics in the following manner:

> Accordingly, whatever is said in reference to a single nature is a single science; for such statements, too, in some way or other, refer to a single subject matter. Clearly, then, the theory of beings as being constitutes a single science.[13]

According to this criterion, there is a science of being *qua* being but since "being" has several meanings, one of which is primary, the science pertains chiefly to that which is primarily named and secondarily to those things that are named in relation to what is first named:

> There is a science which takes up the theory of being as being and of what 'to be' means, taken by itself... Now 'being' has several meanings; but they all have a central reference to some one nature and are not entirely different things that happen to have the same name.[14] ... but they all refer back to a single root: some things are said to 'be' because they are themselves primary beings; others, because they modify primary beings.[15]

What Aristotle claims in these texts about the meanings of "being" depends on the analysis he has made in *Metaphysics* V, chapter seven, where he has distinguished several meanings of "being". Before turning to examine this text, perhaps it is well to pause and consider what Aristotle is attempting to do in metaphysics in order

---

[11] "Next among our general problems is whether a single science deals with all the primary beings." *Met.* III: ch. 2; 997a15-16.
[12] "Next comes the question whether the only primary beings there are, are sensible, or whether there are others." *Ibid.*, 997a35-36.
[13] *Ibid.*, IV: ch. 2; 1003b13-17.
[14] *Ibid.*, ch. 1; 1003a21-22; ch. 2; 1003a32-33.
[15] *Ibid.*, ch. 2; 1003b4-7.

that we may understand his particular purpose in *Metaphysics* V, chapter seven.

4.2   ARISTOTLE'S PURPOSE IN METAPHYSICS

At the end of the *Physics*, Aristotle proves that since motion is eternal, and whatever is in motion is moved by something, there must be a first mover not moved by anything other than itself.[16] A mover of such a nature can be described negatively with reference to the mobile beings that are the subject of natural science: it is indivisible, without parts, and without magnitude:

Now that these points are settled, it is clear that the first unmoved movent cannot have any magnitude. For if it has magnitude, this must be either a finite or an infinite magnitude. Now we have already proved in our course on Physics that there cannot be an infinite magnitude: and we have now proved that it is impossible for a finite magnitude to have an infinite force, and also that it is impossible for a thing to be moved by a finite magnitude during an infinite time. But the first movent causes a motion that is eternal and does cause it during an infinite time. It is clear, therefore, that the first movent is indivisible and is without parts and without magnitude.[17]

With this proof, to be is no longer identified with being material, and natural science — the science of mobile beings — no longer makes claim to be the highest science:

If, then, there is no other primary way of being besides natural being, natural science will be the first science; but, if there is immovable primary being, the science of this will be prior, and first philosophy will thus be general, both because it is first and because it is the theory of beings as being; it examines what is and whatever belongs to beings as being.[18]

This first philosophy, then, is what Aristotle seems to identify when he says, "There is a science which takes up the theory of being as being of what 'to be' means, taken by itself".[19]

[16]   *Physics* VII: ch. 4, 5.
[17]   *Ibid.*, ch. 10; 267b18-26.
[18]   *Met.* VI: ch. 1; 1026a26-32; cf. also XI: ch. 7; 1064b5-12. "...if there is something external and immovable and independent, it is evident that knowledge of it must be theoretical. But this theory does not belong to the natural sciences, since they deal with movable things; not to mathematics; but to a science prior to both." *Met.* VI: ch. 1; 1026a10-13; cf. also IV: ch. 3; 1005a32-b5.
[19]   *Met.* IV: ch. 1; 1003a21-22; see Appendix, p. 91.

From Aristotle's description of the science of being *qua* being, we see that this science should study those things of which "being" can be predicated — the immaterial substances which he has proved to exist as well as all other substances.[20] What is the character of being *qua* being? We have noted in chapter two that scientific knowledge involves the knowledge of the universal.[21] Elsewhere Aristotle describes the unity of a science as dependent on a single genus uniting objects in a single class.[22] So it is that Aristotle regards those terms that both serve as the subject of predication and can be predicated of other things as expressing the subjects of science; there is no science of the individual.[23] Accordingly, therefore, Aristotle considers being *qua* being as the universal subject genus of the science of metaphysics, including all substances:

Furthermore, as any class of things is united in sense perception and in a science (for example, grammar is one science and unites in theory all articulate sounds), so the theoretical science of being as being includes as its parts the sciences of the species of being within the general class of being as being.[24]

[20] It is to the existence of an immaterial substance that St. Thomas refers when he says, "However, in the case of those things which can exist separately, separation rather than abstraction obtains ... Substance, however, which is the intelligible matter of quantity, can exist without quantity. Consequently, the consideration of substance without quantity belongs to the order of separation rather than to that of abstraction." *In Boethium de Trinitate,* V: 3; *The Division and Methods of the Sciences* (Toronto: Pontifical Institute of Mediaeval Studies, 1958), p. 31.

[21] pp. 55-56.

[22] "A single science is one whose domain is a single genus." *Post. An.* I: ch. 28; 87a37.

[23] *Prior An.* I: ch. 27; 43a25-42.

Nich. Eth. VI: ch. 3; 1139b18-24: "Now what *scientific knowledge* is, ... We all suppose that what we know is not even capable of being otherwise; of things capable of being otherwise we do not know, when they have passed outside our observation, whether they exist or not. Therefore the object of scientific knowledge is of necessity. Therefore it is eternal; for things that are of necessity in the unqualified sense are all eternal; ..." The subject of a science is universal and necessary expressed in a universal concept which can be predicated of those particular things to which it is common. Only particular things exist; the universal and necessary as such does not exist. If the universal concept were not predicable of the particular things to which it is common, then there would be no scientific knowledge of existing things.

[24] *Met.* IV: ch. 2; 1003b19-22. "For all substances, insofar as they are beings or substances, pertain to the consideration of this science: but insofar as they

Metaphysics, then, studies all substances as well as accidents.

4.3　THE MEANING OF "BEING"

4.3.1　*Accidental Being and True Being*

In *Metaphysics* IV, chapter two, Aristotle has formulated a criterion
of science:

... whatever is said in reference to a single nature is a single science; ...[25]

To formulate such a criterion is the task of logic which is concerned with the method of philosophy. We notice, too, that this
criterion is formulated in terms of the way in which men speak,
but Aristotle is not speaking merely about language as the subject
of this science. In order to indicate what he means let us turn to
Metaphysics V, chapter seven, where Aristotle is concerned with
the meanings of "being".

In *Metaphysics* IV, chapter two, it has been made clear that
metaphysics as the study of being is concerned with substance and
accidents,

... some things are said to 'be' because they are themselves primary beings;
others, because they modify primary beings;[26] ... any science deals chiefly with
what is primary to its subject, other considerations being derived from and
dependent upon the primary ...[27]

but Aristotle in *Metaphysics* V, chapter seven, gives four meanings
of "being" or the "is" of a predicate:

(1) accidental being: "is" means "happens to be"
(2) essential being: the meanings of "is" correspond to the figures of predication
(3) true being: "is" or "being" signifies the truth of a proposition
(4) "is" signifies actual or potential being

Metaphysics is not concerned, however, with accidental nor with

---

are a certain kind of substance, such as lion or cow, they pertain to the special
sciences." *In Met.* IV: less. 1; #547.
[25]　1003b13.
[26]　1003b5.
[27]　1003b16-17.

true being.[28] Whenever anything is said to be in an accidental sense, the meaning is that (1) both attributes are accidental to the same thing (the just is musical); (2) an attribute is accidental to a being (the man is musical); (3) the attribute belongs to something which is (this musical being is a man). Of accidental being, however, there can be no science, for every science is concerned with what is always or normally so.[29] A systematic account of the extraordinary — what does not happen always or normally — is impossible since the extraordinary has an indeterminate cause; hence a science of the accidental is impossible.[30]

Of true being, Aristotle tells us that the "is" in a statement may mean that the statement is true or false:

> The 'is' in a statement also means that the statement is true; and 'is not', that it is not true, but false ... that Socrates is musical means that this is true, or that Socrates is a nonwhite thing means that this is true; but 'it is not the case that the diagonal of the square is commensurate with the side' means that it is false to say that it is.[31]

"Is" as used in a proposition or expressing a judgment, then, refers to the composition made by the mind. "Being", here, signifies the composition of a proposition which the intellect makes by composing and dividing. It signifies that a proposition — a mental entity — is true. As signifying a mental entity or affection, "is" in this sense must be dismissed as the subject of metaphysics:

> Hence, 'being' ... in the sense of being true must be dismissed ... (it) is something that befalls a mind.[32]

Its cause is an affection of the mind — the operation of the intellect composing and dividing. It does not pertain to the subject of the science of all beings.

Having seen why Aristotle excludes accidental being and being as true from the subject of metaphysics, let us turn to the being of the categories, the subject of metaphysics, to determine both how

[28] Aristotle postpones to Book IX the consideration of actual and potential being which divides the ten predicaments.
[29] *Met.* VI: ch. 2; 1027a20.
[30] *Met.* VI: ch. 4; 1027b30.
[31] *Ibid.*, V: ch. 7; 1017a30-35.
[32] *Ibid.*, VI: ch. 4; 1027b32-35. Parenthesis mine.

Aristotle derives the meanings of "being" from these and how the categories refer to real being outside the mind.

4.3.2 *Essential Being*: *the Being of the Categories*

The meaning of "being" that Aristotle has identified as referring to the subject matter of metaphysics is "being" indicated by the categories. Corresponding to the signification of the predicates are the meanings of "being":

> On the other hand the varieties of essential being are indicated (σημαίνει) by the categories; for in as many ways as there are categories may things be said to 'be'.[33]

In determining the meaning of accidental being, we saw that Aristotle compared a predicate which is an accident with its subject in a proposition.[34] Here, in determining the meanings of being *secundum se* or essential being, Aristotle will examine predicates considered in themselves, as St. Thomas notes.[35] What Aristotle is doing is depending on our human mode of speaking or of predicating concepts to determine the priority of substance to all other categories. What is the reason for Aristotle's dependence on such a method in this context? The overall picture of what Aristotle is attempting to do in metaphysics will assist us in understanding the reasons for his procedure here.

We have noted that Aristotle at the end of the *Physics* has proved the existence of an immaterial mover; thus natural science is not the highest science. Rather, it will be metaphysics that is both the first and highest science as well as the general science of being *qua* being. Metaphysics, then, is the study of all the things of which "being" is predicated, including the immaterial substances. Since to be is not identical with being material, it is not Aristotle's purpose here to determine what material is; that was his purpose in natural science where he could rely on sense observation. His

<hr/>

[33] *Met.* V: ch. 7; 1017a22-23.
[34] cf. *sup.* pp. 82-83.
[35] *In Met.* V: less 9; #885.

purpose rather is to determine what material being *qua* being or substance is. He does this by examining the universal concept of being — the concept in which, as we have seen, the intellect generalizes all reality, both material and immaterial — in order to determine the meaning of being or the meaning of reality. Having done this, it will then be to some degree evident what it means to be an immaterial being. Thus Aristotle will have elucidated the meaning of the subject of his science. The only possible means of examining the meaning of "being" is to examine its use in predication. The first step in the elucidation of the meaning of "being" to determine whether it can be applied to both material and immaterial reality is in *Metaphysics* V, chapter seven. This, then, is the purpose of Aristotle's procedure in this text.[36]

About this procedure St. Thomas notes that the modes of being are consequent on the modes of predicating.[37] How can Aristotle determine the categories of reality from the way men speak? What he is doing is maintaining that we speak the way we do because things are the way they are. This assumes that the knowledge man has of reality is valid and his expression of it in language is accurate. This seems to be the basic assumption of Aristotle's use of language in determining the way things are.

---

[36] St. Thomas refers to this procedure of Aristotle as an examination of the modes of speaking or of predicating (In *Met.* VII: less. 1; #1249). Elsewhere he refers to an examination of predication as a logical method (In VII: less. 2; #1287; less. 3; #1308). Aristotle here does not refer to his method as *logikos*, but he does refer to the method used at VII: ch. 4; 1029b13 and 1030a26 as *logikos*. This method differs from the *logikos* method of Plato who argued from common predicates to the existence of Forms. Aristotle condemns Plato's method at *Met.* XII: ch. 1; 1069a28. For an interpretation of *logikos* method in St. Thomas, see James C. Doig, C.S.C., "Aquinas on Metaphysical Method", *Philosophical Studies* (Maynooth), XIII (1964), 20-34.

Subsequent steps in the clarification of the meaning of "substance" are found in Book VII of the *Metaphysics* where Aristotle, seeing that substance can be used to refer to matter, form, and composite, finally defines substance as essence or essential form, a meaning that can be applied to the Prime Mover. (*Met.* V: ch. 17).

[37] *In Met.* V: less. 9; #890.

Different modes of predicating are not, of course, grammatically distinguished; they are distinguished by different meanings of the predicates. Cf. note 38.

Aristotle has noted that the meanings of "being" correspond to the signification of the predicates. What are the significations of the predicates? In this text of the *Metaphysics*, Aristotle does not explicitly show how he arrives at the categories by examining predicates, but his statement "Since predication asserts (σημαίνει) sometimes what a thing is, sometimes of what sort, ..." indicates how he must have done this. Aristotle's resume of this passage in Book VII indicates that he begins by examining predications made of individual things.[38]

To schematize the figures of predication and to determine the meanings of "being", one must examine the phrases that are predicates in each proposition to determine what they express about a subject.[39] Consider, for example, the following propositions:

(1) Socrates is a man.
(2) Fido is a dog.
(3) Socrates is white.
(4) Callias is brown.
(5) Socrates is good (or bad).
(6) Fido is good (or bad).
(7) Socrates is three cubits tall.
(8) Fido is two cubits long.

If one asks "What is ___?" about each of the predicates in these propositions, one must answer as follows. In the case of propositions (1) and (2), "Man (or dog) is an animal", "Man (or dog) is a living being", Man (or dog) is a substance." Each predicate

[38] "Although 'being' can be used in these various ways, it is evident that of these meanings it is the first that answers the question of what the particular thing designated is; hence it defines 'being' in a primary way. For when we say of what sort a designated thing is, we indicate that it is (for example) good or bad, but say nothing about its being three cubits long or a man; and so, when we tell 'what' a thing is, we do not indicate whether it is white or warm or three cubits long, but that it is (for example) a man or a god. However, the meanings other than primary being are also said to indicate being, because they are in some cases quantities of what a thing is in the primary sense, or its qualities, or what happens to it, or some other feature of that thing's primary being." *Met.* VII: ch. 1; 1028a13-20.

[39] Aristotle indicates that "is" is part of the predicate when he says, "For there is no difference between 'the man *is* getting well', and 'the man gets well'; or between 'the man *is* walking or 'cutting' and 'the man walks' or 'cuts', and so forth." *Met.* V; ch. 7: 1017a28-30.

expresses *what* the subject Socrates or Fido is; "is" expresses the substance of the subject in each case. In the case of (3) and (4), "White (or brown) is a color", "Color is a quality", and "Good (or bad) is a quality", The predicates express of what kind the subject is; "is" expresses the quality of the subject, Socrates, Callias, or Fido. In the cases of (7) and (8), "Three cubits tall (or two cubits long) is a quantity". The predicates express *how much*; "is" expresses the *quantity* of the subject, Socrates or Fido.[40]

Thus it is that Aristotle can say:

> Since predication asserts (σημαίνει) sometimes what a thing is, sometimes of what sort (quality), sometimes how much (quantity), sometimes in what relation (relation), sometimes in what process of doing (action), or undergoing (passion), sometimes where (place), sometimes when, it follows that these are all ways of being.[41]

[40] Trendelenburg holds that the distinctions of categories are derived from grammatical distinctions. We disagree with this opinion for several reasons. First, the noun, verb, conjunction and article were the only parts of speech recognized by Aristotle. Secondly, the categories cut across the grammatical distinctions: quantity and quality both include nouns and adjectives; the categories of time and place are both expressed by adverbs. Aristotle himself was aware of the lack of correlation between the forms of expression and the grammatical categories: "For it is possible for something which is not of the nature of an action to signify by the language used something which is of the nature of an action; for example, to 'flourish' is a form of expression like to 'cut' or to 'build'; yet the former denotes a quality and a certain disposition, the latter an action. So too with the other possible examples." *Soph. Ref.* ch. 4; 166b16-20. Friedrich Adolf Trendelenburg, *Geschichte der Kategorienlehre* (Hildesheim: Georg Olms Verlagsbuchhandlung, 1963), pp. 23-24.

That Aristotle is asking "what is" about the predicates seems clear from his treatment of the categories in the *Topics*: "It is clear, too, on the face of it that the man who signifies something's essence signifies sometimes a substance, sometimes a quality, sometimes some one of the other types of predicate. For when a man is set before him and he says that what is set there is 'a man' or 'an animal', he states its essence and signifies a substance; but when a white colour is set before him and he says that what is set there is 'white' or is 'a colour', he states its essence and signifies a quality. Likewise, also, if a magnitude of a cubit be set before him and he says that describing its essence and signifying a quantity. Likewise, also, in the other cases: for each of these kinds of predicate, if either it be asserted of itself, or its genus be asserted of it, signifies an essence: if, on the other hand, one kind of predicate is asserted of another kind, it does not signify an essence, but a quantity or a quality or one of the other kinds of predicate." I: ch. 9; 103b27-104a1.

[41] *Met.* V: ch. 7; 1017a24-28.

Aristotle lists only eight categories, omitting position and habitus, here in

In the predicate "is a man", "is" expresses substance or *what* the subject is; in "is white", "is" expresses quality; in "is three cubits long", "is" expresses quantity, and so on through all the categories.[42] All that we know about the extra-mental entities can be expressed by predicates categorized in these ten figures of predication.

It is, then, on the basis of this analysis in *Metaphysics* V, chapter seven, that Aristotle announces in *Metaphysics* IV, chapters one and two, the science of being *qua* being as the science primarily of substance and secondarily of accidents.

4.4   THE REFERENT OF "BEING"

We have noted earlier that Aubenque finds no foundation in extra-linguistic reality for the subject of metaphysics. Having observed how Aristotle makes his subject precise, let us conclude by summarizing Aristotle's doctrine of the subject of metaphysics with respect to its referent in reality.

We have seen that Aristotle excludes accidental being as the subject of metaphysics since accidental being refers to a temporary and non-necessary connection in reality about which there can be no science. He also excludes the "being" of judgment which refers to the mental affection, the truth of a proposition. If the being of the categories is the subject of metaphysics, then to what does this "being" refer? How can it be said to refer to real things?

---

the *Metaphysics*, as well as in *Physics*, 225b-9 and *Posterior Analytics*, 83b15. The complete list appears in *Categories*, ch. 4: 1b25 ff and *Topics* I: 103b20 ff.

St. Thomas notes that *per se* being is distinguished from *per accidens* being in terms of *per se* and *per accidens* predication. (In *Met*. V: less. 9; #885). *Per accidens* being is that which is an accidental connection between subject and predicate, such as "The man is musical"; musical man is an accidental being. *Per se* being is expressed by a predicable term which can serve as the subject of a proposition; e.g. "White is a color." "Man is an animal." The division of being into substance and accident, however, is based on the fact that something in its own nature is a substance telling what an individual subject is, or an accident answering of what kind, how much, and so forth.

[42] Cf. *sup.*, note 38.

By an examination of predication, Aristotle notes that some predicates express that the subject is what it is and is not a modification of anything else. For example, "Socrates is a man", "Socrates is an animal", "Fido is a dog". All of these predicates are included under "is a substance". We notice that in these propositions, the concept in subject place refers to extramental reality — Socrates or Fido, as the case may be. The predicate attributes something to the subject, to the extra-mental reality; it expresses what we understand about the subject, that it is a man, a dog, an animal, and so forth.

The predicate, then, is referring to some grasp of the subject; it can refer to several grasps of the same subject inasmuch as the intellect is capable of grasping the subject in many ways: as man, as animal, as white, as good, and so forth. In "Socrates is a man", "man" refers to the humanity of Socrates; in "Fido is a dog", "dog" refers to the dog-nature of Fido; in each of these cases, "is" refers to the subject's being independent of all other things, to his being a particular something by reason of himself; it expresses his substance as *what is*. On the other hand, in "Socrates is white", "white" refers to the modification of color attributed to the substance which is the subject; "is" here refers to the quality of the subject. We see, then, that in saying, "The immaterial mover is a substance", "substance" refers to its being independent of all others and to its being a particular something.

Substance, then, is that which exists independently of everything else in reality; whereas accidents: quantities, qualities, relations and the being of the other categories all exist dependently on substance.[43] Accordingly, the meaning of "being" as said of these categories includes a reference to the "being" said of substance. Aristotle can, therefore, formulate the subject of his science according to the *pròs hén* criterion of a unified science:

---

[43] "We have dealt with primary being; that is, with what 'is' in the primary sense of the word, or with that to which the other categories of being refer. For it is with regard to the concept of primary being that we speak of the being of others, quantity, quality, and so forth; since all of them implicitly, contain a reference to the concept of primary being." *Met.* IX: ch. 1; 1045b26-31.

Accordingly, whatever is said in reference to a single nature is a single science; for such statements, too, in some way or other, refer to a single subject matter. Clearly, then, the theory of being as being constitutes a single science.[44]

But such is not to speak of words or merely to clarify meanings. The foundation in reality, such as Aubenque demands for the science of metaphysics — a demand that is justified by Aristotle's theory of science — is the substances or particular things not insofar as these substances are mobile but insofar as they are existents independent of all else in reality, and secondarily the accidents or modifications of particular things that exist in reality.

4.5. CONCLUSION

Aristotle formulated a *pròs hén* criterion of the unity of a subject of a science. With such a criterion it was necessary for him to make precise the meanings of "being". This procedure, however, does not imply that the meanings of words are the only foundation for his science of metaphysics. In order to determine what we understand by "being" and the corresponding categories of reality, Aristotle examines predication or the way in which men speak. Such a procedure assumes that knowledge of reality acquired by the human intellect is valid and is accurately expressed in language.

The meaning of "being" is derived from the meaning that predicates like "is a man" and "is a dog" manifest when opposed to and compared with predicates like "is white" and "is three cubits tall". The concept in subject place in a predication refers to an extramental individual. What is expressed in the predicate attributes something to the individual; in the case of some predicates the "is" of the predicate expresses substance; in the case of other predicates the "is" expresses some modification of the subject.

Individuals as independent existents are generalized as substances by the intellect and whatever is said with reference to the nature of substance is part of the subject of metaphysics. Individuals may be generalized as men,[45] as animals, as living beings and so forth, but

[44] *Met.* IV: ch. 2; 1003b14-18.
[45] Cf. Chapter II, pp. 41-43.

it is their generalization as substances — independent existents not inhering in anything else — whether material or immaterial that is the concept expressing the subject of metaphysics — being *qua* being.

APPENDIX: THE SUBJECT OF METAPHYSICS

As we have seen, it is clear from Aristotle's text that the existence of an immaterial, eternal being demands a science higher than natural science whose subject is movable being: "The first science, however, is a theory of entities both independent and immovable."[46] Yet it is this science that Aristotle refers to as the universal science of being *qua* being:

... if there is immovable primary being, the science of this will be prior, and first philosophy will thus be general, both because it is first and because it is the theory of being as being; ...[47]

But Aristotle, at this point, gives no explanation why the first science of immovable primary being must also be the general science of being *qua* being. Because of this lack of explanation many interpretations of Aristotle view his theory of the subject of metaphysics as an irreconcilable contradiction between theology and ontology. To these interpretations we will refer later. It is now our purpose to note (1) an explanation found in Aristotle, and (2) a reason why immaterial substance could not be the subject of a science.

Regarding the first point, earlier in Book VI, chapter one, Aristotle, explaining the difference between natural science, mathematics, and metaphysics, notes that the first science is the theory of entities both independent and immovable. He then indicates the important relation of causation between these immaterial entities and other beings:

Though all ultimate factors are necessarily eternal, these objects of first science are especially so, since they explain those divine beings which are accessible to us ...[48]

46 *Met.* VI: ch. 1; 1026a16-17.
47 *Ibid.*, 1026a28-32. Cf. also XI: ch. 7; 1062b9-11.
48 *Ibid.*, VI: ch. 1; 1026a16-18.

This, then, seems to be the explanation for the identity of the science that studies immaterial beings and the science that studies all being. St. Thomas' explanation also seems to be based on the relation of causation between immaterial beings and material beings:

> Because it is first, it is necessary that it is universal. For it is the same science which is about the first beings and which is universal. For the first beings are the principles of the others.[49]

The second point to be considered is the impossibility of immaterial substance being the subject of a science. Before giving reasons for this impossibility, it is necessary to review what Aristotle means by the subject of a science.

If one examines Aristotle's notions of science and of its subject, it becomes clear that according to his own criteria immaterial substances which are the highest causes cannot be the subject of a science. For Aristotle, scientific knowledge is knowledge of the cause on which some facts depends according as it is the cause in such a way that the fact could not be other than it is.[50] The knowledge which is sought through demonstration is a conclusion in which a *per se* property is predicated of some subject of science by inference from prior principles. To have reasoned knowledge about a subject is to know the inherence of an attribute in the subject through a cause. It seems evident, then, that immaterial substances which are the highest causes and have no prior causes cannot be the subject of a science, for how can anything be known about them through their causes.

This impossibility is indicated again in other passages in the *Metaphysics*. In Book VII, chapter seventeen, Aristotle notes that the questions asked about the subject of a science usually ask either for the cause taken as form in matter, or for the cause of the form in matter — the final or efficient causes: "Hence the explanation is sought in terms of the material, that is, that by which it has been definitely formed into a primary being."[51] In other words, to ask "what is" or "why" about something, the essence of that thing must

[49]   *In Met.* XI: less 8; #2267. *Ibid.*, VI: less. 1; #1164-1165.
[50]   *Post. An.* I: ch. 2; 71b8-12.
[51]   *Met.* VII: ch. 17; 1041b7-8.

be complex and known by its matter. The explanation of a fact is always sought in terms of the material. Therefore, Aristotle concludes that there is no inquiry about simple substances which are not composed of matter and form, for in every inquiry there must be something known and an investigation about something whose reason we do not know.[52]

Various interpretations of *Metaphysics* VI, chapter one, view the two statements about the science of metaphysics as first philosophy, as the general science of first philosophy and as the general science of being *qua* being as irreconcilable. Certain interpretations consider this contradiction a result of a revolutionary development in Aristotle's thought. Werner Jaeger[53] holds that Aristotle's earliest theory was that of metaphysics as the science of immaterial substances but that his failure to elaborate this science brought him to a theory of metaphysics as the study of being *qua* being. Sir David Ross[54] considers the two theories of the science of metaphysics irreconcilable, but metaphysics as theology in the dominant theory in Aristotle's thought. Both Jaeger and Ross view Aristotle's theories as undergoing a radical development consequent on his disillusionment with Platonism.

Joseph Owens[55] opines that Aristotle gradually made more precise his meaning of "being *qua* being": from its initial meaning of substance it finally came to mean separated or immaterial being. O. Hamelin[56] agrees that the latter interpretation of the meaning of "being *qua* being" is the correct one. G. L. Muskens[57] holds that in Book VI, chapter one, "being *qua* being" means being in all its extension, while in Book XI, chapter seven, it designates immaterial being.

---

[52] *Met.* IX: ch. 10 shows that since there is no composition in simple beings, one cannot ask those questions about these beings to which science is an answer.
[53] *Aristotle; Fundamentals of the History of His Development*, trans. Richard Robinson. (2nd ed. rev.; Oxford: At the Clarendon Press, 1948).
[54] *Aristotle's Metaphysics* I (Oxford: At the Clarendon Press, 1924), 252-253.
[55] *The Doctrine of Being in the Aristotelian METAPHYSICS* (Toronto: Pontifical Institute of Medieval Studies, 1957), pp. 169-176; 298-299.
[56] *Le système d'Aristote* (Paris: Librairie Félix Alcan, 1931), pp. 405-410.
[57] "De Ente Qua Ens Metaphysicae Aristoteleae Obiecto", *Mnemosyne*, XIII (1947), 130-140.

Augustin Mansion[58] fails to see a radical revolution in Aristotle's theory of the subject of metaphysics but sees rather the reconciliations of the apparently contradictory theories in the causation of being by the first immaterial cause.

On the basis of the explanation we have given at the beginning of this Appendix, we hold that immaterial substance is not the subject of a theological metaphysics in Aristotle's work. Our explanation in chapter four is based on this contention.

---

[58] "L'Objet de la science philosophique suprême d'après Aristotle, Métaphysique, E, 1", *Mélanges de philosophie Grecque offerts à Mfr. Diès* (Paris: Libraire Philosphique J. Vrin, 1956), pp. 161, 167.

Cf. also "Philosophie première, philosophie seconde et metaphysique chez Aristote", *Revue Philosophique de Louvain*, LVI (1958), 180.

Ernest Barker is an interesting case of one who having studied Aristotle's *Politics* in order to write a commentary on it, abandoned the genetic method and the development theory as vitiated by the subjectivity of the particular interpreter's feeling about what should be regarded as "early" and as "late" in a philosopher's development.

Because of this subjectivity the genetic method has often provided different interpreter's with contradictory conclusions. *The Politics of Aristotle*, trans. Ernest Barker (Oxford: At the Clarendon Press, 1946), pp. xli-xlii.

On the genetic method, see also D. J. Allan, *The Philosophy of Aristotle* (London: Oxford University Press, 1952), pp. 14-15.

5

SUMMARY AND CONCLUSION

At the beginning of this work we mentioned several views about whether Aristotle in philosophizing achieved some positive knowledge of reality. To some it seems that he either merely spoke about language or clarified language and thereby dispelled linguistic confusion but did not provide proofs or explanations of anything other than language. Inasmuch as there is no work devoted to the topic of language in Aristotle's philosophy, we undertook what could only amount to the beginning of a study of this vast topic.

To determine whether and how Aristotle achieves positive knowledge of reality, we undertook the investigation of three things: (1) his theory of signification; (2) his theory of philosophical language; (3) one instance of his dependence on language, or on the way men speak, in achieving knowledge of reality. Let us review these investigations.

5.1. THEORY OF SIGNIFICATION

Plato, as we have seen through the Socrates of the *Cratylus*, entertained to a degree the theory of natural names: as instruments names naturally signify the realities or Forms named. An examination of names should reveal whether the Heraclitean or Parmenidean view of reality is the correct one, but such an examination provides no consistent picture of reality. Disappointed in his theory of natural names, Socrates allows convention as a supplement to the natural theory; names signify by unlike sounds as well as by like. But convention will not allow that names are a source of knowledge revealing the true nature of the realities named. So it is that Plato, in his own name in *Letter VII*, expresses his distrust of language which is inadequate to express the true reality.

Aristotle, on the other hand, having rejected the theory of Forms, would not look to names as the source of knowledge of these Forms. The uses of language or power of conversation whereby man is differentiated from the animals are many. Living together, at least for virtuous men, means sharing thought and discussion. Inasmuch as the rational principle may be used theoretically, practically, or artistically, the object of understanding and communication will vary accordingly. On one practical level, the possibility of signifying the just and the unjust, the useful and the injurious is the basis for the domestic and civil societies to which man naturally belongs. The wise man who has leisure from practical affairs interests himself in knowledge for its own sake. He uses language to signify the basic factors and principles of things and to communicate this knowledge. Finally, the literary artist needs language both to relate the thoughts of a character to his action and to present the action of a plot. These, then, are the uses of language which make a man not only a political and social being but allow him to be contemplative and artist.

Giving language its foundation in thought or intelligence, Aristotle speaks of words as the symbols of mental experiences which are the signs of things. Men all have the same speech sounds and mental experiences, but the words symbolizing these mental experiences may differ from one locality to another. If words are symbols and not signs, then they are significant by the conventions of men and not naturally; nothing is by nature a name, for letters and syllables have no natural likeness to the objects named. Natural inarticulate sounds designate states of emotion but do not signify; only lettered names are symbols, constituted intelligently with a definite meaning.

Meaning, for Aristotle, is the property of a word whereby it arrests the attention and communicates understanding. But meaning is a property not only of words but also, of course, of sentences.

Aristotle, however, in his logic is interested only in those sentences that express truth and falsity — enunciations. Logical meaning, then, in a more restricted sense, is the property of enunciations expressing truth and falsity. Meaning is a property also of the parts of the sentence — the name and the verb — but these are properly defined on logical grounds, according as they are the subjects or predicates of enunciations or predications. Words that are not properly names and verbs but are cases of names and verbs include (1) tense, number, and voice of verbs, (2) genders and cases, singular and plural forms of nouns, and (3) adjectives and adverbs derived from the nouns. The other meaningless words used in sentences — articles, conjunctions, pronouns — have a limited sense of meaning insofar as they have a function when used with names and verbs in a sentence.

It was easy to see, then, that although Aristotle gives a general theory of meaning as a property that arrests the attention and communicates understanding, his elaboration of meaning and significance is directed to the method of philosophy — logic as it is concerned with enunciations. Because of this, one cannot at this point claim that Aristotle's interest in language was a grammatical one of formulating the general rules of correct speech.

Before concluding, however, that Aristotle's interest in language is not grammatical, we examined the *Poetics* and the *Rhetoric*, two works in which he makes formal statements about language. The examination of these works indicated (1) that in both *Poetics* and *Rhetoric* Aristotle is not interested primarily in language but in the formulation of the argument of the plot and of the arguments whereby the rhetorician persuades his audience; (2) in the *Rhetoric*, Aristotle gives a brief, inadequate and negative treatment of five points of pure and correct Greek; (3) in both works, because style is important for the instruction and pleasure of the audience, Aristotle treats of linguistic style, but this is proper not to language in general but to oratory and to poetry.

Having seen that Aristotle is interested not in grammar but in logic, i.e. the method of philosophy concerned with the causes and principles of real things, we next turned to the terms which are particularly relevant for philosophy. Since the subject of science must be universal and necessary, abstracted from particulars, universal terms are those of prime importance for philosophy. To what do these universal terms refer? A simple expression such as "man" symbolizes the universal in the mind but refers indirectly to the common characteristics in men from which the universal has been apprehended.

There remained for us to determine what further specifications Aristotle makes regarding language in philosophy.

5.2. PHILOSOPHICAL LANGUAGE

We have seen that general terms referring to universals are the subject terms of philosophy, but Aristotle makes further precisions about the language used in philosophy. He speaks of philosophical language as the language of proof. In this section of our work we endeavored to determine the meaning of "language or proof" and the kinds of words admitted by Aristotle in philosophical proofs.

Aristotle rejects Hesiod and accepts Empedocles as a philosopher on the basis of language. What is the difference in the use of language by each of these predecessors of Aristotle? Hesiod, we pointed out, used fables expressed in terms referring to mythical entities in order to solve his problem: the eternity of the gods. Empedocles, on the other hand, posed his problem and its solution in terms that refer to real things: love and strife explain the eternity of the universe and of God. But while his explanation referred to real principles, Empedocles used either a metaphor or a confused term in his explanation. His task, nevertheless, was viewed by Aristotle as a philosophical one undertaken in a philosophical manner. We see, then, that the first criterion of philosophical language is that it must refer not to fictional principles but to real things.

We next turned to the question of what Aristotle could mean by "proof" in "language of proof". Aristotle refers to "proof" as *apodeixis*. Strictly speaking, this term refers to the demonstration that is productive of scientific knowledge. Yet Aristotle uses it to refer to dialectical and rhetorical proofs productive of only probable conclusions as well as poetic arguments that something is or is not the case. Not all of these proofs are admitted in speculative philosophy which, unlike rhetoric, aims not to persuade an uninstructed audience regarding the contingent matter of human actions but to attain knowledge of the causes of reality. For the purpose of speculative philosophy, demonstrative and dialectical proofs are those upon which Aristotle relies to attain knowledge of reality.

We noted that by "language of proof" Aristotle refers to the dialectical and demonstrative proofs of speculative philosophy. We then asked what restrictions Aristotle makes regarding the language of these proofs. Aristotle speaks of the use of common words in rhetoric and poetry. We have shown that these common words include foreign words made ordinary by custom and metaphors that have been naturalized by common use. It is by the use of common words that clarity, the fundamental point of style, is achieved; yet the diction of rhetoric and poetry cannot be commonplace. To achieve the balance of clarity without banality, the rhetorician is allowed the use of metaphor while the poet uses not only metaphor but rare and ornamental words also.

On the other hand, in dialectical and demonstrative arguments clarity prohibits the uses of metaphor — the application of a strange term to name that for which it is not commonly used. One may define what Aristotle means by clarity in these arguments as the lack of equivocation, ambiguity and metaphors. Equivocation and ambiguity are avoided by specifying the definite meanings of words that have several meanings. In this way one may be certain that arguments are directed to the same point. Clarification of language is made by the philosopher in order that his words may be directed to a definite referent.

We then turned to notice Aristotle's attitude to some of his predecessors regarding clarification of meanings. Aristotle refused to admit the Sophists as philosophers because they purposely did not distinguish meanings of words but engaged in linguistic sleight.

Not to have a specific meaning, for Aristotle, is to have no meaning; it is to refer to nothing. Plato, too, failed to distinguish the meanings of "being" in searching for the causes of all things. Aristotle, therefore, views it as the first task of the metaphysician to distinguish the senses in which things may be said "to be".

Besides confused meaning, Aristotle forbids the use of metaphors which we have shown to be a mode of equivocation in philosophy. Plato used a metaphorical sense of "to come from" to explain the relation of Ideas and sensible things; he gave no new meaning for this new usage. To avoid equivocation, the meaning of any word should refer definitely to that which it is properly imposed to name. Because metaphor is used in ordinary conversation, we concluded that for Aristotle, philosophical language will not be as broad in scope as the language of ordinary conversation. It is not in order to make his language like that of ordinary conversation that the philosopher clarifies words.

Having seen the meaning of confused terms and metaphor, we returned to Empedocles' use of "love and strife" to refer to the principles of unity and disunity both among men and in the cosmos. If Empedocles made no distinction between the universe and men, he used a confused term. If he did make such a distinction and was drawing an analogy, the application of "love and strife" to the forces of the universe is a metaphor. In either case, although Empedocles used explanation by real principles, his "language of proof" did not yet fulfill Aristotle's criteria.

Having seen that clarity in philosophical arguments means the avoidance of equivocation and ambiguity including metaphor, we asked whether only univocal words may be used in philosophy. Aristotle distinguishes a third type besides the univocal word and the equivocal: words said in many ways in which different senses are derived from and related to a prior meaning; hence these are called *pròs hén* equivocals. The criterion of *pròs hén* equivocals is that the primary meaning is implicit in the definitions of all secondary meanings because there is some relation between the things named. As we pointed out, different relations occur in different instances of *pròs hén* equivocals, but in virtue of *any* relation the primary definition or meaning is included in the definition or meaning of the thing to which the name is secondarily imposed. The fact that this criterion of *pròs hén* words is not introduced every time Aristotle refers to equivocals in general does not, we argued, indicate necessarily that in some part of his career Aristotle was not aware of *pròs hén* equivocals. Particularly in the *Sophistical Refutations* and the *Topics*, Aristotle is concerned with the necessity of specification of definite meanings if the fallacy of equivocation is to be avoided; this specification of meanings applies equally to coincidental equivocation and to *pròs hén* equivocals.

We concluded that what Aristotle refers to as equivocation or as words said in many ways (πολλαχῶς λεγόμενα) includes two kinds: (1) equivocation by chance, and (2) words related *pròs hén*. Both kinds are referred to by the generic names of either equivocation or πολλαχῶς λεγόμενα.

Aristotle uses the term "metaphor" in such a way that the term itself is a *pròs hén* equivocal. The term "nature" is used metaphorically to signify every substance. This meaning is included among the *pròs hén* meanings of "nature" that refer to the first meaning and that are used in metaphysics. It seems, then, that "metaphor" is itself a *pròs hén* equivocal broad enough to include as species both *pròs hén* equivocals and metaphor in the strict sense. Actually, every *pròs hén* equivocal is a metaphor in the loose sense of an *extended* term.

Another example of the use of "metaphor" inclined us to disagree with Boethius' division of words for Aristotle as (1) univocals, (2) equivocals by chance, and (3) equivocals by design or *pròs hén* equivocals. "Power" as used in geometry is an extension or metaphor from "power" in the sense of active potency. As such, it is surely not an equivocal by chance; neither, however, is it a *pròs hén* equivocal since its definition does not refer to the primary meaning of "power". It seems, then, that Boethius' division of equivocal by design or *pròs hén* equivocal can be broadened to include not only *pròs hén* equivocals but also metaphorical words which are not equivocals by chance but whose definitions do not include a reference to the definition of the word from which they were originally extended.

At the beginning of this section we asked the meaning of philosophical language as the language of proof. We immediately saw that the language of proof excludes terms that refer to fictional entities. Secondly, unlike poetry and rhetoric, dialectical and demonstrative proofs of philosophy exclude the use of metaphors to name things which their meanings do not signify. Yet philosophy admits of more than univocal terms. *Pròs hén* equivocals may be used to name related realities; such equivocals have the advantage of drawing attention to the relationship between the realities that they name, e.g., substance, quantity, and quality called "beings" and a surgeon and an instrument called "medical". Such *pròs hén* equivocals, however, do not escape the need for precise and definite meaning if the words are to be used properly and the fallacy of equivocation is to be avoided. In excluding the use of metaphors from philosophical arguments, we noted that at the same time Aristotle uses "metaphor" to cover generically every extension of a term, including *pròs hén* equivocals.

5.3. A USE OF LANGUAGE: THE MEANING OF "BEING"

In the last section of our work it was our purpose to examine an instance of Aristotle's use of language in order to indicate how he was concerned not solely with linguistic clarification but with positive knowledge of non-linguistic reality. Having seen in the earlier parts of our work that Aristotle has a theory of signification in which words are symbols of concepts which are signs of things, that Aristotle claims to be concerned with finding the principles and causes of real things, and that he is dissatisfied both with the use of fictions as principles of explanation and with explanations by means of words whose meanings do not clearly refer to definite things, we turned to Aristotle's establishment of the subject of metaphysics unified according to a linguistic criterion in order to assess Aristotle's use of language in determining the meaning of the subject of this science.

But first we claimed that according to the texts of Aristotle and contrary to some interpretations of them, metaphysics is the first and general science of being *qua* being. After the discovery of the immaterial mover, being no longer can be identified with being material, and physics is not the highest science. It is the science of the immovable and primary being which Aristotle is trying to elaborate in metaphysics. This science, we claimed, studies all the things of which "being" can be predicated but not without restrictions as we notice in examining *Metaphysics* V, chapter seven.

In *Metaphysics* IV, chapter two, Aristotle adds to the criterion of the unity of a science which he has given in *Posterior Analytics* a further specification, "Whatever is said in reference to a single nature is a single science". According to this, metaphysics will be the science of substance and whatever is said in relation to substance. It is in *Metaphysics* V, chapter seven, however, that Aristotle distinguishes the meanings of "being" that pertain to the subject of metaphysics.

Aristotle claims four meanings of "being". Of these, two do not pertain to real being — accidental being which refers to a non-necessary connection in reality and true being which refers to a mental affection. These two meanings of "being" do not refer to real being and so are eliminated from metaphysics. The division of being into actual and potential being is postponed until Book Nine. What Aristotle is concerned with is the meaning of "being" that pertains to the subject of metaphysics.

These meanings of "being" correspond to the categories which Aristotle determines by examining the predicates of material being in order to determine the meaning of material being *qua* being. The basic assumption of this entire procedure is that man has valid knowledge of reality accurately expressed in language. We speak the way we do because things are the way they are.

The modes of being, therefore, are determined from the modes of predication — from the common meaning of predicates. These modes of predication are determined by examining the way men speak: by asking "what?" of each of the predicates of real being. The ultimate answers are the ten categories: substance, quantity, quality, relation, action, passion, place, time, (although position and habitus are omitted in this listing). All that we know about extra-mental reality is expressed by predicates classed in these ten figures of predication.

Contrary to Aubenque, then, we claimed that Aristotle had a non-linguistic foundation for being *qua* being — the referent of "substance" and the nine categories. The subject to which the predicates examined are attributed refers to an extra-mental reality. What the predicates such as "is an animal", "is a man" have in common is that they refer to the subject's being something by reason of itself, to its being independent of other things; the "is" of such predicates signifies substance. Predicates such as "is white", "is three cubits tall" refer not to the independence of the subject but to some modification of it; the "is" of these predicates signifies some modification of a substance.

"To be" primarily means to be independent of other things, to be something by reason of itself, to be a substance. Secondarily, it means the different modifications of substance: what sort of substance, how much, in what relation, in what process of doing or undergoing, where, when. This, then, is the positive knowledge that Aristotle offers of reality: to be is to be something independent of other things. By examining the way men speak, Aristotle determines what they understand by "to be". What they understand is the positive aspect of reality.

BIBLIOGRAPHY

PRIMARY SOURCES

Aristotle, *The "Art" of Rhetoric*. Translated by John Henry Freese (Cambridge: Harvard University Press, 1926).
——, *The Eudemian Ethics*. Translated by H. Rackham (Cambridge: Harvard University Press, 1952).
——, *Metaphysics*. Translated by Richard Hope (Ann Arbor: Ann Arbor Paperbacks; University of Michigan Press, 1960).
——, *The Poetics*. Translated by W. Hamilton Fyfe (Cambridge: Harvard University Press, 1927).
The Basic Works of Aristotle. Edited and with an Introduction by Richard McKeon (New York: Random House, 1941).
The Politics of Aristotle. Translated with notes by Ernst Barker (Oxford: At the Clarendon Press, 1946).
The Politics of Aristotle. Edited by W. L. Newman, Vol. II. (Oxford: At the Clarendon Press, 1887).
The Works of Aristotle. Translated into English under the editorship of J. A. Smith and W. D. Ross. Vol. I: *Categoriae and De Interpretatione, Analytica Priora, Analytica Posteriora, Topica and De Sophisticis Elenchis* (Oxford: At the Clarendon Press, 1928).
The Works of Aristotle. Translated into English under the editorship of J. A. Smith and W. D. Ross. Vol. IV: *Historia Animalium* (Oxford: At the Clarendon Press, 1910).
The Works of Aristotle. Translated into English under the editorship of J. A. Smith and W. D. Ross. Vol. V: *De Partibus Animalium, De Motu and De Incessu Animalium, De Generatione Animalium* (Oxford: At the Clarendon Press, 1912).
The Works of Aristotle. Translated into English under the editorship of W. D. Ross. Vol. VII: *Problemata* (Oxford: At the Clarendon Press, 1927).
The Works of Aristotle. Translated into English under the editorship of W. D. Ross. Vol. X: *Politica, Oeconomica, Atheniensium Republica* (Oxford: At the Clarendon Press, 1921).
Plato, *The Collected Dialogues of Plato*. Edited by Edith Hamilton and Huntington Cairns (New York: Pantheon Books, 1961).

106   BIBLIOGRAPHY

COMMENTARIES

Aristotle, *Organon*, 5 vols. Translated by J. Tricot (Paris: Librairie Philoso-phique J. Vrin, 1936).

Aristotelis Organon Graece. Edited by Theodorus Waitz (Lipsiae: Sumtibus Hahnii, 1844).

Aristotle, *Categories and De Interpretatione.* Translated by J. L. Ackrill (Ox-ford: At the Clarendon Press, 1963).

Aquinas, St. Thomas, *In Duodecim Libros Metaphysicorum Aristotelis Expositio.* Edited by M. R. Cathala, O. P. and R. M. Spiazzi (O. P. Tairomo: Marietti, 1950).

——, *In Octo Libros Physicorum Aristotelis Expositio.* Edited by P. M. Mag-giolo (O. P. Taurini: Marietti, 1954).

——, *In Aristotelis Libros Peri Hermeneias Et Posteriorum Analyticorum Expo-sitio.* Edited by R. M. Spiazzi (O. P. Taurini: Marietti, 1955).

Boethius, *In Categorias Aristotelis. Patrologiae Cursus Completus.* Edited by J. P. Migne (Paris, 1852).

Butcher, S. H., *Aristotle's Theory of Poetry and Fine Art.* 4th ed. revised (Dover Publications, Inc., 1951).

Bywater, Ingram, *Aristotle on the Art of Poetry* (Oxford: At the Clarendon Press, 1909).

Colle, Gaston, *La Métaphysique*, vol. IV (Louvain: Editions de l'institut supérieur de philosophie, 1931).

Cope, Edward Meredith, *The Rhetoric of Aristotle with a Commentary.* 3 vols (Cambridge: At the University).

Else, Gerald F., *Aristotle's Poetics: The Argument* (Cambridge: Harvard Uni-versity Press, 1957).

Ross, W. D., *Aristotle's Metaphysics* (Oxford: At the Clarendon Press, 1924).

——, *Aristotle's Prior and Posterior Analytics* (Oxford: At the Clarendon Press, 1949).

Twining, Thomas, *Aristotle's Treatise on Poetry* (London: Payne and Son, 1789).

BOOKS

Allan, D. J., *The Philosophy of Aristotle* (London: Oxford University Press, 1952).

Anscombe, G. E. M., and Geach, P. T., *Three Philosophers* (Ithaca: Cornell University Press, 1961).

Aubenque, Pierre, *Le probleme de l'Etre chez Aristote* (Paris: Presses Universi-taires de France, 1962).

Bonitz, H., *Index Aristotelicus.* 2nd ed. revised (Graz: Akademische Druck-u. Verlaganstalt, 1955).

Brentano, Franz, *Von der mannigfachen Bedeutung des Seienden nach Aristoteles* (Hildesheim: Georg Olms Verlagsbuchhandlung, 1960).

Charlesworth, Maxwell John, *Philosophy and Linguistic Analysis* (Pittsburgh: Duquesne University, 1959).

Cope, E. M., *An Introduction to Aristotle's Rhetoric* (London and Cambridge:

Macmillan and Co., 1867).

Cornford, F. M., *From Religion to Philosophy*: A Study in the Origins of Western Speculation (New York: Harper & Bros, 1957).

Décarie, Vianney, *L'Objet de la métaphysique selon Aristote* (Paris: Librairie Philosophique J. Vrin, 1961).

Dufrenne, Mikel, *Language and Philosophy*. Translated by Henry B. Veatch (Bloomington: Indiana University Press, 1963).

Gilson, Etienne, *L'Etre et l'essence* (Paris: Librairie Philosophique J. Vrin, 1948).

Grene, Marjorie, *A Portrait of Aristotle* (London: Faber and Faber Limited, 1963).

Hamelin, O., *Le système d'Aristote* (Paris: Librairie Felix Alcan, 1931).

Jaeger, Werner, *Aristotle*; *Fundamentals of the History of His Development*. Translated by Richard Robinson. 2nd ed. revised (Oxford: At the Clarendon Press, 1948).

Kapp, Ernst, *Greek Foundations of Traditional Logic* (New York: Columbia University Press, 1942).

Kirk, G. S. and Raven, J. E., *The Presocratic Philosophers* (Cambridge: At the University Press, 1957).

Kneale, William, and Kneale, Martha, *The Development of Logic* (Oxford: At the Clarendon Press, 1962).

LeBlond, J. M., *Logique et méthode chez Aristote* (Paris: Librairie Philosophique J. Vrin, 1939).

Lukasiewicz, Jan, *Aristotle's Syllogistic from the Standpoint of Modern Formal Logic* (Oxford: At the Clarendon Press, 1951).

McInerny, Ralph M., *The Logic of Analogy*; *An Interpretation of St. Thomas* (The Hague: Martinus Nijhoff, 1961).

Ogden, C. K. and Richards, I. A., *The Meaning of Meaning* (New York: Harcourt, Brace and World, 1923).

Owens, Joseph, *The Doctrine of Being in the Aristotelian Metaphysics* (Toronto: Pontifical Institute of Medieval Studies, 1957).

Peck, Harry Thurston, *History of Classical Philology* (New York: The Macmillan Co., 1911).

Rijk, Lambertus Marie de, *The Place of the Categories of Being in Aristotle's Philosophy* (Assen: Van Gorcum, 1952).

Robins, Robert Henry, *Ancient and Medieval Grammatical Theory in Europe* (London: Bell, 1951).

Ross, W. D., *Aristotle*. 3rd ed. revised (London: Methuen & Co., 1937).

Sandys, John Edwin, *A History of Classical Scholarship*. Vol. I: *From the Sixth Century B.C. to the End of the Middle Ages* (Cambridge: At the University Press, 1908-1921).

Snell, Bruno, *The Discovery of Mind*: *The Greek Origins of European Thought*. Translated by T. G. Rosenmeyer (Cambridge: Harvard University Press, 1953).

Steinthal, H., *Geschichte der Sprachwissenschaft bei den Griechen und Roemern*. 2 vols (Berlin: Ferd. Duemmlers Verlagsbuchhandlung, 1890).

Trendelenburg, Friedrich Adolf, *Geschichte der Kategorienlehre* (Hildesheim: Georg Olms Verlagsbuchhandlung, 1963).

ARTICLES

Berry, Kenneth K., "Relation of Aristotelian Categories to Logic and Meta-physics", *New Scholasticism*, XIV (1940), 406-411.
Doig, James C., C.S.C., "Aquinas on Metaphysical Method", *Philosophical Studies*, XIII (1964), 20-36.
Hayakawa, S. I., "What Is Meant by Aristotelian Structure of Language?", *Language, Meaning and Maturity*. Edited by S. I. Hayakawa (New York: Harper & Brothers, 1954), pp. 217-224.
Landesman, Charles, "Does Language Embody a Philosophical Point of View?", *Review of Metaphysics*, XIV (June, 1961), 617-636.
Louis, Pierre, "Observations sur le vocabulaire technique d'Aristote", *Mélanges de philosophie grecque offerts à Mgr. Diès* (Paris: Librairie Philosophique J. Vrin, 1956), pp. 141-149.
Macdonald, Margaret, "The Philosopher's Use of Analogy", *Logic and Language*. Edited by Antony Flew (Oxford: Basil Blackwell, 1955), pp. 80-100.
McInerny, Ralph M., "Metaphor and Analogy", *Sciences Ecclésiastiques*, XVI (Mai-Septembre 1964), 273-289.
——, "Notes on Being and Predication", *Laval Theologique et Philosophique*, XV (1959), 236-274.
——, "Some Notes on Being and Predication", *Thomist*, XXII (July, 1959), 315-335.
Mansion, Augustin, "L'Objet de la philosophique suprême d'après Aristote, Métaphysique, E, 1". in *Mélanges de philosophie grecque offerts à Mgr. Diès* (Paris: Librairie Philosophique J. Vrin, 1956), pp. 151-168.
——, "Philosophie première, philosophie seconde et métaphysique chez Aristote", *Revue Philosophique de Louvain*, LVI (1958), 165-221.
Muskens, G. L., "De Ente Qua Ens Metaphysicae Aristoteleae Obiecto", *Mnemosyne*, XIII (1947), 130-140.
Owen, G. E. L., "Logic and Metaphysics in Some Earlier Works of Aristotle", *Aristotle and Plato in the Mid-Fourth Century*. Edited by I. Duering and G. E. L. Owen (Goetenburg: Almquist & Wiksell, 1960), pp. 163-190.
——, "Τιθέναι τα Θαινόμενα", in *Aristote et les problèmes de méthode* (Louvain: Publications Universitaires, 1961), pp. 83-103.
Owens, J., "Aristotle on Categories", *Review of Metaphysics*, XIV (Sept., 1960), 73-90.
Ryle, Gilbert, "The Theory of Meaning", in *The Importance of Language*. Edited by Max Black (Englewood Cliffs: Prentice-Hall, 1962).
Trépanier, Emmanuel, "Philosophes et grammairiens sur la définition du verbe", *Laval Théologique et Philosophique*, XVII (1961), 87-99.

INDEX

accidents, 71, 82; see 'categories'
Ackrill, J. L., 23-24, 29
action, 87, 104
adjectives, 32, 97
adverbs, 97
Aeschylus, 57
Allan, D. J., 94n
ambiguity, 60-61, 76, 99-102; see
   'equivocation', 'confused meaning'
analogy, 48-49
   argument from, 52
   and metaphor, 66
analytical science, 50
apodeictic language, see 'language of
   proof,'
ἀπόδειξις, 49-53, 54, 98-99
aporiae, 78
argument, 42, 97
   linguistic (*logikos*), 12
   poetical, 39, 44, 52-53, 99
   rhetorical, 39, 44, 52-53
   see 'proof'
article, 27-28, 32, 33, 97
Aubenque, Pierre, 9, 11, 78n., 88, 104

Barker, Ernest, 94n
being
   accidental, 82-84, 88
   actual or potential, 82, 83n.
   essential, 82, 84-88
   per accidens, 88n.
   per se, 88n.
   true, 82-84, 88
   see 'substance', 'accidents', 'categories'

"being", meanings of, 9, 10, 11, 64, 79,
   82-88, 90-91, 100, 102-104
being *qua* being, 9, 78-79, 80-82, 84-
   85, 91-92, 93-94, 103-104
beings, mobile, 80
Boethius, 75, 75n., 101
Bonitz, H., 26n.
Bywater, Ingram, 26n., 32n., 38n.,
   56n., 59n.

cases
   of nouns, 29, 33, 35, 97
   of verbs, 32, 33, 35, 97
categories, 42, 43, 83-88, 88-90, 90-91,
   103
   see 'substance', 'accidents'
Categories, 28, 29, 61, 68, 70n., 88n.
cause, knowledge of, 92-94
Charlesworth, Maxwell John, 10, 78n.
clarity, see 'language'
conjunctions, 27-28, 32, 33, 97
convention, 13, 15-17, 22-24, 26, 33
   36, 96
conviction, 50, 52
Cope, John Meredith, 37n., 52n., 58n.,
   59n.
Cornford, F. M., 48n.
Cratylus, 10, 13, 14, 22, 22n., 23, 24,
   25n., 36n., 95
custom, 15, 23, 57

De Anima, 18n.
definitions, 54
   and clarity, 61-64, 64-67

see 'equivocals'
De Generatione Animalium, 18n., 68n.
De Interpretatione, 14, 14n., 21n., 22n., 26n., 27n., 28, 28n., 29n., 30n., 31n., 32n., 36, 39, 44
demonstrative proofs, 49-53, 61-62, 76, 99-102;
see 'proofs'
denotation, 35
De Partibus Animalium, 18n.
De Sensu, 18n.
dialectical proofs, 49-53, 61-62, 76, 99-102
see 'proofs'
diction,
in iambic poetry, 59
in ordinary conversation, 59
in poetry, 57-61
in rhetoric, 57-61
Dionysius Thrax, 36
Doig, James C., 85n.
During, I., 69n.

Else, Gerald F., 37
Empedocles, 25n., 46-49, 64-67, 98, 100
enthymemes, 38, 39, 51-53, 61
enunciations, 33, 39, 97
equivocals
ab uno, 75-76
a casu, 75-76, 101
a consilio, 75-76, 101
according to a similitude, 75-76
according to a proportion, 75-76
ad unum, 75-76
coincidental, 67-72
derived from different prior meanings (*pròs hén*), 68-72, 72-75, 75-76, 77, 89, 90, 100-102
equivocation, 60-62, 72-75, 99-102
see 'ambiguity', 'confused meaning'
etymology, 15, 17
Eudemian Ethics, 68n., 69n.
Euripides, 57
examples, 38, 39, 51-53, 61
extension of meaning
see 'metaphor'
fables, 48, 52

see 'myths'
fictional elements, 47-49
figures of speech, 38
Forms, 16, 17, 18, 95-96
see 'Ideas'
friendship,
see 'love and strife'

gender, 97
general terms, signification of, 40-43
Gilson, Etienne, 31, 31n.
grammar, 11, 13, 35-40, 97

habitus, 103
Hamelin, O., 93
"health", 70-72
Hecuba, 53
Helen, 53
Hesiod, 11, 46-49, 98
Historia Animalium, 18n., 28n.
history, 40
Homer, 11

Ideas, 64, 66
immaterial being, 84, 91-94, 103
In De Interpretatione, 21n., 23n., 27n., 29n., 30n., 31n.
induction, 53
In Metaphysicorum, 47, 73n., 74n., 82n., 84n., 85n., 88n., 92
intelligence, 21, 23, 25
"is", 83, 86n
see 'being'

Jaeger, Werner, 93

Kirk, G.S., 48n.

language, 18-19
as communication, 19, 20, 22, 24, 25;
See 'speech,' 'meaning,' 'signification'
clarification of, 78-79, 99
clarity of, 54-61, 99
in art, 19-21, 96
in practical matters, 19-20, 96
of myths or fables, 49

philosophical, 9, 11, ch.3 *passim*, 95, 98-102
language of proof, 11, 12, ch.3 *passim*, 98-100;
see '*apodeixis*'
Letter VII, 14, 17, 95
logic, 35-40, 49-53, 82, 97
logikos method, 85n.
logos, 19n.
love and strife, 47-49, 98, 100

Macdonald, Margaret, 9
McInerny, Ralph M., 73n.
Mansion, Augustin, 94
mathematics, 91
meaning,
 clarity of, 61-62
 confused, 54-55, 62-64, 100; see "equivocation," 'ambiguity'
 in poetry and rhetoric, 55-61
language and, 19, 21-25, 33, 43-44, 96-98
 of parts of sentences, 27-28
 of sentences, 25-27
 philosophical, 13, 43-44, 55
 primary meaning of a word, 69, 75-76, 101
 secondary meaning of a word, 75-76, 101
 see "signification"
Menelaus, 53
mental experience, 21, 34, 96
metaphor, 56-61, 64-67, 72-75, 99-102
metaphysics, 9, 10, 12, 77, 80-84, 84-88, 88-91, 91-94, 102-104
Metaphysics, 10, 11, 12, 19n., 20, 41n., 42n., 43n., 45, 46, 47n., 63n., 64n., 66n., 68n., 69n., 71, 72, 73n., 74n., 75n., 78, 78n., 79, 79n., 80n., 81n., 82-84, 82n., 83n., 84n., 85n., 86, 87n., 88n., 89n., 90n., 91n., 92n., 93, 93n., 103
modes of persuasion, 51
Muskens, G.L., 93
mythologists, 11, 34, 48, 49
myths, 38, 46, 48

names, 14-18, 19n., 31-33, 31n., 34-35, 54-55, 97

arbitrary, 24
as communicating meaning, 17
as images, 15
as imitations, 15, 17, 24-25
natural relation to things, 10-12, 13-18, 22-24, 95
see 'words,' 'language'
naming
 as an action, 14
 as an instrument of teaching, 14
natural science, 80, 91
nature, 48
"nature," meanings of, 41, 72-75, 101
Nichomachean Ethics, 19n., 20, 41n., 42n., 81n.
nouns, 27-30, 31, 35, 39, 59, 97;
 see 'ὄνομα'

ὄνομα, 19n., 22n., 29n., 56n., 33
ontology, metaphysics as, 91-94
ordinary conversation, 67
ordinary words, 56-61, 61-62
Organon, 55
ornamental language, 38, 39
Owen, G.E.L., 69n., 72
Owens, Joseph, 93

Parmenides, 64
parts of speech, 38-40
passion, 87, 104
perception, 41-42
philosophical language, 9, 11, ch.3 *passim*, 95, 98-102
philosophy, 45, 54-55, 61-67, ch.4 *passim*,
 differs from poetry and history, 40-41
 speculative and practical, 41
 see 'knowledge of reality'
philosophical meaning
 see 'meaning'
phrase, 29, 33
 non-predicative, 26
 predicative, 26
 significant, 26
Physics, 41n., 53n., 54n., 64.n, 78n., 80, 80n., 84, 88n.

physis
  see 'nature'
place, 87, 104
Plato, 10, 14, 17, 22n., 35, 62, 63, 63n.,
  64, 65, 66, 85n., 100
Poetics, 19n., 21n., 25n., 26n., 27n.,
  28n., 29, 30n., 31n., 32n., 37, 38,
  38n., 39, 40n., 41n., 44, 53n., 55n.,
  56n., 57n., 58n., 59n., 60, 60n., 61,
  72, 73, 74, 97
poetry, 24-25, 35-40, 41, 97
Politics, 18n., 20n.
position, 104
Posterior Analytics, 41n., 42n., 49n.,
  50n., 65n., 81n., 88n., 92
"potency" meanings of, 73-74
"power," meanings of, 74-75, 101
predication, 26n., 31, 32, 33, 42, 81,
  84-88, 88-90, 90-91, 97, 104
  literal, 67
  metaphorical, 67
  per accidens, 88n.
  per se, 88n.
predecessors of Aristotle, 45, 46, 62,
  72
principles of real things, 46-47, 63-64,
  77-78, 96, 97
Prior Analytics, 42n., 51n., 61, 81n.
pronouns, 27-28, 32, 33, 97
proofs 98-99, 46-49; see 'demonstrative proofs,' 'dialectical proofs'
propositions, 26, 27, 31, 32, 33, 83, 86;
  see 'enunciations'
Protagoras of Abdera, 35

quality, 87-88, 88-90, 102, 104
quantity, 87-88, 88-89, 102, 103

Raven, J.E., 48n.
reality, 9, 10, 41, 43
  Heraclitean view of, 15, 95
  knowledge of, 11, 12, 13-17, 35, 53,
  78, 84-85, 95-96, 102
  Parmenidean view of, 95
referent, 11, 34-35, 36, 40, 43, 44, 49,
  63, 101
  of "being," 88-90
relation, 89, 104

rhetoric, 35-40, 50-53, 97
Rhetoric, 24, 25n., 35n., 37, 37n., 38n.,
  39, 41n., 44, 48n., 50n., 51n., 52n.,
  55n., 56n., 58n., 59n., 60, 61, 97
Robins, Robert Henry, 26n., 36n., 40
Ross, Sir David, 93

Sandys, John Edwin, 35n.
science
  subject of, 81, 91-94, 98
  unity of, 79, 81, 82, 88-90, 103
scientific knowledge, 41-43, 49-53, 81,
  92-94, 99
sentences, 29, 32, 33, 97
  commands, 26, 27, 35
  meaning of, 25-27
  parts of, 27-28
  prayers, 26, 27, 35
  propositions, see 'enunciations'
signification, 13-18, 21-33, 77, 95
  of general terms, 40-43
  see 'convention,' 'meaning,' 'names'
Socrates, 13, 14, 15, 16, 17
Sophist, 22, 36n.
Sophistical Refutations, 10, 35n., 54n.,
  62n., 63n., 69n., 70, 70n., 87n., 101
Sophists, 62-64, 67, 70
sound, 14, 18, 19
  articulate, 18, 19n., 96
  inarticulate, 23, 96
  significant, 27
  without meaning, 27
  see 'voice'
speech
  power of, 19
  see 'language,' 'voice'
strife, see 'love and strife'
style, 55-61
  clarity, 57; see 'clarity'
  in poetry and prose, 37-40, 44
  perspicuity in, 58
  use of common words, 58
substance, 81-82, 82-84, 84-88, 90-91,
  101-102, 103;
  see 'categories'
syllables, 14
symbols, words as, 10, 21, 22, 24, 25,
  33, 54, 96

syncategorematic words, 28

Techné Grammatiké, 36
tense, 97
theologians, 46, 49
theology, metaphysics as, 91-94
time, 104
Topics, 19n., 35n., 50n., 62n., 65n.,
68n., 69n., 70, 70n., 71, 87n., 88n.,
101
Trendelenburg, Friedrich Adolf, 87n.
Trepanier, Emmanuel, 31n.
Tricot, J., 43n.
Twining, Thomas, 56n., 57n., 59n.

universals, 40-43, 81
univocal terms, 45, 64-67, 67-72, 75-
76, 100-102

verb, 27-28, 29, 30-33, 35, 37, 39
as name, 29n., 31

indefinite, 32
signifies with time, 30
voice, see 'sound'

Waitz, Theodorus, 32n.
what is, 87-88, 90-91, 103
when, 87
words
altered, 57
common, 57, 99
curtailed, 57
foreign (unfamiliar), 56, 58
invented, 57
lengthened, 57
metaphorical, 57
(see 'metaphor')
ordinary, 56-61, 61-62
ornamental, 57
proper, 57
see 'name,' 'equivocals,' 'univocals'